I AM WOMAN, HEAR ME SNORE

Other Cathy® Books from Andrews McMeel Publishing

Abs of Steel, Buns of Cinnamon
Understanding the "Why" Chromosome
The Child Within Has Been Awakened But the Old Lady on the Outside Just
Collapsed
Revelations from a 45-Pound Purse
Only Love Can Break a Heart, But a Shoe Sale Can Come Close
$14 in the Bank and a $200 Face in My Purse
My Granddaughter Has Fleas!!
Why Do the Right Words Always Come out of the Wrong Mouth?
A Hand to Hold, an Opinion to Reject
Thin Thighs in Thirty Years
Wake Me Up When I'm a Size 5
Men Should Come with Instruction Booklets
A Mouthful of Breath Mints and No One to Kiss
Another Saturday Night of Wild and Reckless Abandon

Cathy Twentieth Anniversary Collection
Reflections: A Fifteenth Anniversary Collection

I AM WOMAN, HEAR ME SNORE

A *Cathy* Collection by Cathy Guisewite

Andrews McMeel
Publishing

Kansas City

Cathy® is distributed internationally by Universal Press Syndicate.

I Am Woman, Hear Me Snore copyright © 1998 by Cathy Guisewite. All rights reserved. Printed in the United States of America. No part of this book may be used or reproduced in any manner whatsoever without written permission except in the case of reprints in the context of reviews. For information, write Andrews McMeel Publishing, an Andrews McMeel Universal company, 4520 Main Street, Kansas City, Missouri 64111.

www.andrewsmcmeel.com

98 99 00 01 02 BAH 10 9 8 7 6 5 4 3 2 1

ISBN: 0-8362-6821-0

Library of Congress Catalog Card Number: 98-85336

Cathy® may be viewed on the Internet at:
www.uexpress.com

─── **ATTENTION: SCHOOLS AND BUSINESSES** ───

Andrews McMeel books are available at quantity discounts with bulk purchase for educational, business, or sales promotional use. For information, please write to: Special Sales Department, Andrews McMeel Publishing, 4520 Main Street, Kansas City, Missouri 64111.

WHAT IF THE FDA APPROVES THE NEW ANTI-FAT PILL AND **ALSO** APPROVES THE NEW NON-FAT FAT, CATHY?

WILL WE TAKE THE ANTI-FAT PILL AND EAT NORMAL FAT ...OR SKIP THE PILL AND JUST EAT NON-FAT FAT?

WHAT ARE YOU TALKING ABOUT, CHARLENE?

WE'LL TAKE THE ANTI-FAT PILL **AND** EAT NON-FAT FAT AND HAVE OUR BODIES SO PROGRAMMED AGAINST FAT THEY WON'T EVEN NOTICE WHEN WE SLIDE IN THE REAL FUDGE BROWNIES!

I LOVE DINING WITH A VISIONARY.

THE GREAT THINKERS ARE ALWAYS A FEW STEPS AHEAD OF SCIENCE.

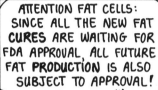

ATTENTION FAT CELLS: SINCE ALL THE NEW FAT CURES ARE WAITING FOR FDA APPROVAL, ALL FUTURE FAT PRODUCTION IS ALSO SUBJECT TO APPROVAL!

NO NEW FAT MAY BE CREATED OR DISTRIBUTED UNTIL SAID APPROVAL IS GRANTED!

ANY FAT PRODUCED WITHOUT APPROVAL WILL BE DESTROYED IMMEDIATELY!!

POINK!

...IT'S TOUGH TO BE THE GOVERNING BODY WHEN YOUR BODY'S DOING THE GOVERNING...

"IN THE PAST TEN YEARS, THE AMOUNT OF MONEY SPENT ON DIET PROGRAMS HAS DOUBLED TO $35 BILLION A YEAR."

"IN THE EXACT SAME TEN-YEAR PERIOD, ADULT AMERICANS HAVE GAINED AN AVERAGE OF EIGHT POUNDS EACH."

"THE MORE MONEY WE SPEND DIETING, THE MORE WEIGHT WE GAIN...THE MORE WEIGHT WE GAIN, THE MORE MONEY WE SPEND DIETING...."

WHEN THEY SPEAK OF THE MILLENNIUM, THEY'RE REFERRING TO THE FUTURE SPAN OF OUR WAISTLINE.

"THE TRIPLE-DECKER PIZZA WITH HAM..."
"THE DOUBLE SUPREME CHEESEBURGER..."
"THE FOUR-POUND MACHO BURRITO MEAL..."
"THE BACON CHEESEBURGER DOUBLE-DECKER TACO...."

IS AMERICA REBELLING AGAINST COUNTING FAT GRAMS WITH THIS EXPLOSION OF CHEESE-STUFFED, BACON-SMOTHERED, GREASE-DRIPPING, COLOSSAL-SIZED FAST FOOD....

...OR HAVE WE SIMPLY FOUND A MORE EFFICIENT WAY TO FEEL PETITE?

LOOK HOW TEENY MY HAND LOOKS NEXT TO THIS GIANT TUB OF FRIES!

FRIES

AS A NATION, WE'RE FATTER THAN WE WERE BEFORE DIET SODA WAS INVENTED. HOW DEPRESSING IS THAT ??

WE'RE FATTER THAN WE WERE BEFORE THERE WAS LOW-FAT YOGURT, LOW-FAT SALAD DRESSING, LOW-FAT GRANOLA, LOW-FAT MAYONNAISE AND LOW-FAT MUFFINS!

WE'VE OBSESSED OVER EACH MISERABLE LOW-FAT, NON-FAT, ARTIFICIALLY SWEETENED LITE BITE OF FOOD AND **LOOK AT US!! LOOK WHERE WE ARE NOW!!!**

IN LINE FOR A DOUBLE-BACON-CHEESE-BURGER DELUXE.

ALSO A MILK-SHAKE. WE WERE THINNER WHEN WE USED TO DRINK MILKSHAKES.

JUMBO MEAL

TODAY IS THE DAY I RECLAIM CONTROL OF MY CAREER!

...EXCEPT I CAN'T GET THE ZIPPER UP ON MY POWER SUIT.

TODAY IS THE DAY I RADIATE CONFIDENCE AND FEMININITY NO MATTER WHAT SIZE I AM!

...EXCEPT MY SKIRTS ARE ALL TOO TIGHT.

TODAY IS THE DAY I LIVE FOR THE MOMENT, NOT FOR WHO I PLAN TO BE IN THE FUTURE!!

EXCEPT THERE'S NOTHING IN THIS STUPID CLOSET THAT FITS!!

LIFE ISN'T A DRESS REHEARSAL. IT'S A SWEATSUIT REHEARSAL.

RECEPTION

DIARY OF A HEALTHY LIFESTYLE
1. CLEANSED MY HEALTHY SKIN.
2. BRUSHED MY HEALTHY HAIR.
3. ATE MY HEALTHY BREAKFAST.

4. POWER-WALKED MY HEALTHY FEET, HEALTHY NAILS, HEALTHY GUMS, HEALTHY MAJOR MUSCLE GROUPS AND HEALTHY ATTITUDE TO THE CAR.

5. DROVE CAR TO COFFEE SHOP. BOUGHT AND ATE A CHOCOLATE CHIP CROISSANT.

THE HYPE CAN GET ME OUT THE DOOR, BUT IT CAN'T GET ME THROUGH THE DAY.

I'VE BEEN DISGUSTED WITH YOU FOR YEARS... ...OF **COURSE** YOU CHOSE TODAY TO BE PERFECT!

TODAY, WHEN I HAVE AN APPOINTMENT TO GET RID OF YOU, YOU'RE BEING EXACTLY THE WAY I ALWAYS DREAMED YOU COULD BE!

DO I CANCEL THE APPOINTMENT, BELIEVE YOU'VE CHANGED, AND HAVE YOU MAKE A FOOL OF ME AGAIN LATER ??... OR DO I CUT YOU OFF THE VERY MOMENT THERE APPEARS TO BE NEW HOPE FOR US??

AAUGH!!

GOD GAVE US HAIR AS TRAINING TO LIVE WITH MEN.

OH, HI, DOLL! YAK, YAK! YOU LOOK **FABULOUS**!

...EXCUSE ME... ARE YOU PAYING ATTENTION TO HOW YOU'RE CUTTING MY HAIR?

KISS, KISS! MAURICE! HOW **ARE** YOU? KISS, KISS!

MY HAIR... YOU'RE NOT CONCENTRATING ON MY HAIR...

YAK YAK KISS KISS YAK KISS KISS YAK

THAT **DOES** IT! EVERYONE OUT! ALL KISSING, YAKKING FRIENDS GO OUT!!!

...THERE. SEE? ISN'T IT BETTER WHEN YOU CAN FOCUS ON WHAT YOU'RE DOING ??

1970s:
THE POWER PERM.
SUCCESSFULLY RE-CREATED
ON 9,999,999 OUT OF
10,000,000 WOMEN.

1980s:
THE SASSY BOB.
SUCCESSFULLY RE-CREATED
ON 9,999,999 OUT OF
10,000,000 WOMEN.

1990s:
THE SEXY, TOUSLED LOOK.
SUCCESSFULLY RE-CREATED
ON 9,999,999 OUT OF
10,000,000 WOMEN.

SOME HAIR HAS DEAD ENDS. MY HAIR IS A DEAD END.

Row 1:

PULL ON BANGS WITH FULL STRENGTH OF ARM AND CEMENT THEM TO FOREHEAD WITH HAIR SPRAY.

CHOP RANDOM HAIRS FROM BACK OF HEAD AND TRY BRAIDING THEM INTO BANGS TO ADD LENGTH.

PILE ALL REMAINING HAIR ON TOP OF HEAD AND DRAPE IT OVER FACE.

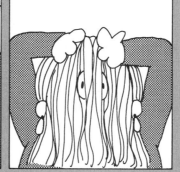

THE MARK OF A GREAT HAIRCUT... YOU CAN DO SO MUCH WITH IT.

Row 2:

CHARLENE: CUT OFF ALL SYMPATHY BECAUSE I REFUSE TO TAKE OFF MY HEADBAND AND SHOW HER HOW BAD MY SHORT BANGS LOOK.

NO HUMILIATION, NO PITY.

ANDREA: CUT OFF ALL CONSOLATION BECAUSE SHE CAN'T STAND THE NEGATIVE STEREOTYPE OF WOMEN WHO OBSESS OVER THEIR HAIR.

GET A LIFE.

LYNDA, CHERYL AND PAT: CUT OFF ALL COMMISERATION BECAUSE THEY ALL THINK THEIR HAIR LOOKS WORSE AND ARE SICK OF ME WHINING ABOUT MINE.

HAH!

A WEEK AFTER THE HAIRCUT, AND PARTS OF MY LIFE ARE STILL BEING CHOPPED OFF.

Row 3:

IT'S SPRING AND THE BODY PART OF THE SEASON IS...

DON'T SAY **BUST!** I CAN'T TAKE ANY MORE BUST!!

JUST DON'T SAY **THIGHS** LIKE 1994!

NO! THIGHS WERE '93. **TUMMIES** WERE '94! DON'T SAY TUMMIES! **ANYTHING** BUT TUMMIES!!

THE BODY PART OF THE SEASON IS THE **HIPS!**

AACK!! NOT THE **HIPS!!** THE HIPS INVOLVE THE TUMMY **AND** THIGHS AND MUST BE BALANCED BY A BIG BUST!!

FASHION'S FINALLY ADDRESSING THE WHOLE WOMAN!

WHEN IS IT THE BIG TOE'S TURN?...

Panel 1: LAST SPRING WAS THE "RETURN TO GLAMOUR", REMEMBER? IMPECCABLE LITTLE SUITS...REFINED LITTLE PUMPS AND BAGS...

Panel 2: YES...WELL, DID THE ROYAL FAMILY INVITE US TO HIGH TEA?...NO! DID WE RECEIVE ANY BOX SEATS TO WIMBLEDON?...NO!

Panel 3: DID WEARING A PUSHUP BRA AND GIRDLE GET US ANY CLOSER TO LUNCHEON ABOARD THE PRIVATE YACHT OF A NEUROSURGEON?...NO!

Panel 4: THEREFORE, WE'RE BACK TO DRESSING LIKE SLOUCHES?

IF WE'RE GOING TO BE UNAPPRECIATED, WE MIGHT AS WELL BE COMFY.

Panel 5: I SPENT A FORTUNE ON THIS SUIT LAST YEAR BECAUSE YOU CONVINCED ME WE'D ENTERED THE ERA OF ELEGANCE. IS THE ERA OVER ALREADY??

Panel 6: NO! IT JUST LOOSENED UP! SEE?... SIMPLY LOSE THE STUFFY LITTLE BELT...TRADE THE UPTIGHT SKIRT FOR A NEON FRUIT-PRINT SARONG ...TOSS ON A STRIPED TEE...

Panel 7: ...SWITCH THE "I'M TRYING TOO HARD" STILETTOS FOR SOME LOW-KEY BUCKLE PUMPS... AND VOILA! ELEGANCE IS SOMETHING YOU CARRY ON THE INSIDE!

Panel 8: ...IN THE RECEIPT COMPARTMENT OF MY WALLET.

P.S. YOU'LL NEED A CLASHING TOTE FOR ALL THE MAKEUP YOU WON'T BE WEARING.

Panel 9: WOMEN ARE SPENDING LESS ON CLOTHES AND MORE ON HOME FURNISHINGS. WE KNOW THIS.

Panel 10: SO, THIS YEAR WE HAVE GORGEOUS FLORAL WALLPAPER PRINT SKIRTS... ...DEN SOFA-TYPE STRIPED PANTS...SHOWER CURTAIN SWIRL MINIS... POLKA-DOTTED SHEER DRAPERY MATERIAL BLOUSES....

Panel 11: FOR LESS MONEY AND WAY MORE VERSATILITY, YOU CAN BUY FABULOUS, FUN NEW CLOTHES, LEAVE THEM LYING ALL OVER THE PLACE AND VOILA... ...YOU'VE REDECORATED!!

Panel 12: CATHY!

HOLD ON! THIS DRESS COULD COMPLETELY UPDATE MY LIVING ROOM CHAIR!

DID YOU HAUL YOUR SHOPPING BAG STUFFED WITH RECEIPTS TO THE ACCOUNTANT YET, CATHY?

MOTHER, PLEASE. I HAVE A COMPUTER NOW.

THIS YEAR I SIMPLY HAVE TO INSTALL MY NEW TAX PREP SOFTWARE...STUDY THE INSTRUCTION BOOK...FIND A SOFTWARE HOTLINE REP... ...FIND THE IRS WEB SITE... ...DOWNLOAD ANSWERS TO MY QUESTIONS... ACCESS THE ELECTRONIC FILING PATH...

AND THEN WHAT?

THEN I HAUL THE SHOPPING BAG STUFFED WITH RECEIPTS TO THE ACCOUNTANT!

WE'RE PROUD OF YOU, DEAR.

WE DON'T KNOW WHY, BUT WE'RE PROUD OF YOU.

9:00 PM: CONNECTED TO IRS WEB SITE TO CHECK QUESTION ABOUT TAX FORM.

9:06 PM: EXPLORED JUPITER ON NASA WEB SITE.
9:20 PM: READ LETTERMAN'S "TOP 10" LISTS FOR JANUARY.
9:33 PM: CHECKED WEATHER IN FIJI.
9:46 PM: WANDERED AROUND LOUVRE.
10:15 PM: JOINED CHAT ROOM DISCUSSING BEET FARMING.
10:35 PM: PLAYED ONLINE SCRABBLE WITH COUPLE IN TOLEDO.
11:35 PM: VISITED LIBRARY OF CONGRESS.
12:19 AM: DOWNLOADED RECIPE FOR LOW-FAT GUACAMOLE.
12:30 AM: VISITED HOME PAGE OF GIRL SCOUT TROUP.
12:45 AM: ORDERED SIX CD'S AND AN EVENING GOWN.
1:10 AM: HAD TAROT CARDS READ.

1:30 AM: LOGGED OFF THE PROCRASTINATION SUPER HIGHWAY.

"THE THEME OF THE IRS FOR 1996 IS HELP. PRE-RECORDED TAX HELP 24 HOURS A DAY...LIVE PHONE HELP 10 HOURS A DAY... HELP AT WALK-IN OFFICES.. ..VIDEO HELP...ONLINE HELP..."

MISC. RECEIPTS

"HELP IN CHEERY SOUND-BITES...HELP IN HIP, FOUR-COLOR GRAPHICS...HELP FOR ABSOLUTELY, POSITIVELY EVERY SINGLE TAX QUESTION YOU MAY HAVE!!"

WILL SOMEONE COME TO MY HOME AND ORGANIZE ALL MY STUFF FROM LAST YEAR?

SORRY. CAN'T HELP YOU.

ONLY THE GOVERNMENT COULD SPEND $7 BILLION OVERLOOKING THE OBVIOUS.

MISC. RECEIPTS

OF THE ZILLION TAX REFORMS PLANNED, THE ONLY THING THAT ACTUALLY GOT DONE WAS MOVING THE MAILING LABEL FROM THE OUTSIDE TO THE INSIDE OF FORM 1040??

CORRECT! AND OF THE ZILLION PERSONAL REFORMS **YOU** PLANNED, THE ONLY THING **YOU** ACTUALLY DID WAS BUY A BIGGER PURSE TO STUFF RECEIPTS INTO!

SEE?? THE GOVERNMENT IS JUST LIKE YOU! JUST A WHOLE BUNCH OF INDECISIVE, WEAK-WILLED, PROCRASTINATORS LIKE YOU!

WE WANTED A GOVERNMENT **BY** THE PEOPLE AND **FOR** THE PEOPLE! WE DIDN'T WANT A GOVERNMENT **LIKE** THE PEOPLE!!

SAVINGS WERE SPENT. AN ETERNITY PASSED. SAVINGS ARE STILL GONE.

BANGS WERE CUT OFF. AN ETERNITY PASSED. BANGS ARE STILL GONE.

WEIGHT WAS LOST SIX MINUTES PASSED. WEIGHT IS BACK IN FULL.

HOW IRONIC THAT INSTANT REJUVENATION ONLY OCCURS IN FAT.

BETWEEN YOUR NEW COMPUTER, SOFTWARE, MODEM AND PRINTER, YOU SPENT $3700 FAILING TO DO YOUR INCOME TAX RETURN YOURSELF, CATHY....

...WHEREAS **I**, YOUR HUMBLE ACCOUNTANT, ACTUALLY **DID** THE RETURN FOR A MERE...

$175??!! THAT'S AN OUTRAGE!! THAT'S ROBBERY!! $175?!!

HOW REASSURING TO KNOW THE SPOTLIGHT WILL CONTINUE TO SHINE ON THE C.P.A.'S.

I DEMAND BACKUP FOR EVERY DIME YOU CHARGED ME!!

ACCOUNTANT

Panel 1: AS A BUSINESS PERSON, I'M WELL AWARE OF THE CURRENT TRENDS OF CORPORATE DOWNSIZING, BUYOUTS AND RESTRUCTURING, DAD.

Panel 2: I KNOW ALL ABOUT TECHNOLOGY'S IMPACT ON JOB SECURITY AND THE SERIOUS NEED FOR LONG-RANGE FINANCIAL PLANNING AS WE MOVE INTO AN INCREASINGLY UNCERTAIN FUTURE.

Panel 3: THANK HEAVENS, HONEY. WHAT KIND OF INVESTMENTS HAVE YOU MADE?

OH, I'M LEAVING THOSE DETAILS UP TO MY POTENTIAL FUTURE HUSBAND, THE PRINCE, AND OUR STAFF OF COURT ADVISERS.

Panel 4: THAT'S THE PROBLEM WITH THE SOLID TWO-PARENT FAMILY. SHE LISTENED TO BOTH OF US.

Panel 5: OF **COURSE** YOUR GENERATION SAVED MORE, MOM...

Panel 6: YOU AND DAD COULD BUY A NEW CAR FOR WHAT I HAD TO PAY FOR A BIG-SCREEN TV...

EGGS

Panel 7: YOU COULD BUY 25 GALLONS OF MILK FOR WHAT I SPEND ON A BOTTLE OF SHAMPOO... YOU COULD STAY IN A HOTEL FOR FOUR NIGHTS FOR WHAT I PAY FOR A PAIR OF PANTYHOSE!

Panel 8: AACK!! YOU PAY $15 FOR A PAIR OF PANTYHOSE??!

IF YOU KNOW YOU CAN'T WIN, DRIVE THE COMPETITION FROM THE ROOM.

Panel 9: EVERY MONTH SIMON AND I PUT A LITTLE ASIDE FOR A COLLEGE FUND...A LITTLE ASIDE FOR A NEW HOUSE FUND...A LITTLE ASIDE FOR A RETIREMENT FUND ...AND A LITTLE ASIDE FOR A VACATION FUND.

Panel 10: YOU PUT MONEY ASIDE FOR ALL THAT EVERY MONTH??

OF COURSE!

Panel 11: THEN WE SCOOP UP ALL THE MONEY WE PUT ASIDE, DUMP IT ON THAT MONTH'S BILLS...AND IF THERE'S $20 LEFT, WE RUN OUT AND SPEND IT AS FAST AS WE CAN IN SHEER DISGUST!!

Panel 12: VERY IMPRESSIVE.

GRANDMA HAD A NEST EGG. WE HAVE A STAINLESS STEEL OMELETTE PAN.

COME ON, BABY... SHOW ME THE BRADFORD FILES!...

...NO! SWEETHEART! NOT THE ERROR BOX! YOU WERE MAKING PIE CHARTS FOR ME TEN MINUTES AGO, AND NOW EVERYTHING I DO IS WRONG! HONEY... PLEASE!!

YOUR COMPUTER IS FINE, MR. PINKLEY. SHE JUST HAS PMS TODAY.

BLEAH! DIDN'T HEAR THAT! DIDN'T HEAR THAT!

IF MEN CAN'T COPE WITH THE WHOLE PACKAGE, WHY DO THEY TURN ALL THEIR MACHINES INTO GIRLS?

IT'S SECRETARIES' DAY, AND YET, WHICH OF US IS REALLY A "SECRETARY" ANYMORE?

WE'RE TELECOMMUNICATIONS DIRECTORS WITHOUT THE BIG SALARY... DATA ANALYSTS WITHOUT THE BIG SALARY... ...PERSONNEL MANAGERS, COMPUTER TECHS AND IN-HOUSE THERAPISTS WITHOUT THE BIG SALARY....

IN SHORT, THE ONLY THING REMOTELY "SECRETARIAL" ABOUT THE POSITION IS THE PUNY PAYCHECK!

ALSO, WE ALL CHIPPED IN TO BUY YOU A NICE GREETING CARD!

TO TRADITION!

QUICK! MY DAUGHTER'S COMING TO WORK TODAY! LET ME HIDE ALL MY JUNK FOOD IN YOUR OFFICE!

QUICK! MY DAUGHTER'S COMING TO WORK TODAY! LET ME HIDE THIS MESS IN YOUR OFFICE!

QUICK! MY DAUGHTER'S COMING! LET ME HIDE ALL THE GARBAGE THAT'S BEEN HEAPED ON MY FLOOR IN YOUR OFFICE!

NO CHILDREN... AND YET PROFOUNDLY CONNECTED TO THE GLOBAL VILLAGE...

BLEAH! HOW CAN SHE WORK IN THAT PIG STY, MOMMY?

DO YOU EVER WORRY ABOUT... YOU KNOW... JOB SECURITY HERE?

SHH! ARE YOU **CRAZY**?! DON'T LET **THAT** VIBE GET OUT IN THE AIR!!

IF THEY THINK **YOU** THINK YOU MIGHT GET DUMPED, **THEY'LL** START THINKING ABOUT DUMPING YOU!

EVEN IF THEY DON'T **WANT** TO DUMP YOU, THEY'LL **CONSIDER** DUMPING YOU JUST BECAUSE BY THINKING "DUMP" YOU HAVE BECOME **DUMPABLE**!!

QUICK! SQUIRT SOME ROOM DEODORIZER! NEUTRALIZE THE CONCEPT!

OUR SINGLE FRIENDS ADD SO MUCH INSIGHT TO LIFE.

WHEN I COULDN'T GET THROUGH THE GLASS CEILING, I SQUIRTED IT WITH WINDEX...

Secretaries Week

WHEN THE MACHINES DESIGNED TO REPLACE ME TOOK OVER HALF MY DESK, I STUCK HAPPY LITTLE SAYINGS ALL OVER THEM...

AND WHEN THIS TOP-HEAVY BARGE OF A BUSINESS SINKS FROM EXECUTIVE COMPENSATION PACKAGES, I'LL BE STANDING RIGHT THERE WITH MY SNORKEL AND WATER-VAC....

...WHICH I'LL TOSS INTO THE GURGLING MUCK SO THE MEN CAN CLEAN UP THEIR OWN MESS FOR ONCE!!

YOU CAN'T BE AN OPTIMIST WITHOUT HAVING A DREAM.

YOU QUIT WEARING YOUR HEADBAND, CATHY. YOUR BANGS MUST HAVE FINALLY GROWN OUT.

I QUIT WEARING THE HEADBAND LAST WEEK, CHARLENE.

OH. I DIDN'T NOTICE.

THE HEADBAND WAS ALL I THOUGHT ABOUT FOR A MONTH! HOW COULD YOU NOT NOTICE??

I JUST DIDN'T NOTICE.

WITH EVERY BREATH I TOOK I WAS FIXATED ON THE POSITION OF THE HEADBAND! YOU **HAD** TO NOTICE WHEN IT CAME OFF!

DID ANYONE NOTICE??

NOTICE WHAT?

HONESTLY... PEOPLE ARE SO SELF-ABSORBED...

I MET HIM IN AN ONLINE CHAT ROOM. HE SENT ME E-MAIL. DO I E-MAIL HIM RIGHT BACK, OR DO I WAIT AND APPEAR COY?

IF I E-MAIL RIGHT AWAY, AND THEN HE DOESN'T E-MAIL ME AGAIN RIGHT AWAY, DOES IT MEAN I E-MAILED TOO QUICKLY? DID I ALREADY WAIT TOO LONG? ARE WE ALREADY IN CYBER-WEIRDNESS??

DO THE SAME RULES APPLY TO ONLINE RELATIONSHIPS, OR IS THERE SOME WHOLE NEW SECRET SET OF RULES THAT WE CAN ONLY FIGURE OUT THROUGH A BRAND NEW SERIES OF PERSONAL HUMILIATIONS?!!

..."USER FRIENDLY," INDEED.....

YOU MET SOMEONE?? WHAT'S HE LIKE??

ACCORDING TO HIS ONLINE PROFILE, HE'S A SENSITIVE, 38-YEAR-OLD PHARMACIST, MOM....

...OR, HE COULD BE A BODY-BUILDER PRETENDING TO BE A PHARMACIST... OR A KID PRETENDING TO BE A GROWN-UP... OR A WOMAN PRETENDING TO BE A MAN... OR A MARRIED PERSON PRETENDING TO BE SINGLE... OR A COMPLETE GEEK PRETENDING TO BE MR. FABULOUS...OR....

SHE MET SOMEONE!!

YOU WERE SUPPOSED TO CALL WHEN THINGS GOT THIS DESPERATE, DAD.

I HAD INSTRUCTIONS TO NOT TIE UP YOUR PHONE LINE, HONEY.

Dear Cathy,
  I already feel closer to you than any woman I've ever known. I love how we can open up to each other online without the complications of physical involvement. May our love grow, and may we never be tempted to ruin it by actually meeting each other in person. Love, H.

SQUIRT

KISS

I HATE THE '90s.

28

WHAT DOES HE LOOK LIKE, CATHY?

THAT'S THE BEAUTY OF ONLINE DATING, CHARLENE. LOOKS DON'T MATTER.

HAIR DOESN'T MATTER. WEIGHT DOESN'T MATTER. FACES DON'T MATTER.

ALL THAT MATTERS IS GETTING TO KNOW A REAL HUMAN BEING THROUGH THE BEAUTIFUL, MEANINGFUL WRITTEN WORD!!

WHAT DO YOU TWO WRITE ABOUT?

WE'RE TRYING TO FIGURE OUT HOW TO DOWNLOAD PICTURES OF EACH OTHER.

YOU'RE DATING SOMEONE NEW, CATHY??

I MET HIM ON THE INTERNET. WE TALKED ONLINE UNTIL 3:00 THIS MORNING!

OH. SO YOU'RE NOT REALLY DATING.

WE TALKED UNTIL 1:00 am YESTERDAY, AND UNTIL 2:00 am THE DAY BEFORE THAT!

WE'RE INVOLVED! CONNECTED! A CRITICAL PART OF EACH OTHER'S LIVES!

BUT YOU'RE STILL NOT DATING.

HOW MANY ONLINE HOURS MUST I LOG BEFORE IT COUNTS AS ONE DATE??!

WHEW! YOU'RE GETTING CRANKY! BETTER START GOING OUT WITH SOMEONE.

HOWARD ISN'T IN OUR USUAL CHAT ROOM... MAYBE HE SNEAKED INTO A DIFFERENT ROOM SO HE COULD MEET SOMEONE ELSE...

MAYBE HE MET SOMEONE AND WENT IN A PRIVATE CHAT ROOM... MAYBE HE'S JUMPING FROM ROOM TO ROOM... MAYBE HE'S USING AN ALIAS SCREEN NAME SO EVEN IF I SEE HIM I WON'T RECOGNIZE HIM....

AACK! JEALOUSY SUSPICION PARANOIA AACK!!

NOTHING LIKE A LITTLE TOUCH OF THE OLD WORLD TO MAKE THE NEW FRONTIER FEEL LIKE HOME....

Panel 1: LET'S SEE HOW ACCURATE YOU WERE IN YOUR ONLINE DESCRIPTION OF YOURSELF TO HOWARD. — WHAT DO YOU MEAN BY "ACCURATE"?

Panel 2: DID YOU TELL HIM HOW YOU CURRENTLY LOOK? — WHAT TIME FRAME ARE YOU USING FOR "CURRENT"?

Panel 3: CURRENT! NOW! THIS MINUTE! "IN THE RAPIDLY CHANGING LIFE OF A WOMAN, WHICH OF US CAN EVER PINPOINT HOW WE LOOK AT ANY GIVEN MINUTE VERSUS HOW WE **COULD** LOOK AT SOME OTHER GIVEN MINUTE??!"

Panel 4: "PERFECTLY TONED SIZE 5." — I DROVE PAST THE GYM ON MY WAY HOME THAT NIGHT. IT WAS ALL WITHIN MY GRASP.

Panel 5: WHICH ONE IS HE? WHICH ONE IS HE? — RIGHT THERE! SEE, MOM? HE JUST SAID "HI"!

Panel 6: WHERE? I JUST SEE A SCREEN FULL OF WORDS. — IT'S AN ONLINE PUBLIC CHAT ROOM. THERE ARE LOTS OF CONVERSATIONS GOING ON AT ONCE...

Panel 7: SEE? THERE HE IS. THAT'S HIS SCREEN NAME AND THAT'S MY SCREEN NAME, AND THAT'S HIS "HI." "HI" TO ME! SEE??

Panel 8: HE TYPES SO BEAUTIFULLY! — SHE'S A TROUPER, DAD. — SHE'S A MOTHER, HONEY.

Panel 9: IF YOU WANT TO KNOW IF HE WROTE, JUST CHECK YOUR E-MAIL AGAIN! — CAN'T. IT'S BAD ROMANTIC KARMA TO CHECK E-MAIL MORE THAN EVERY 17 MINUTES.

Panel 10: ANSWERING MACHINES CAN BE CHECKED EVERY 14 MINUTES...VOICE MAIL CAN BE CHECKED EVERY 8 MINUTES...BUT THE ODDS OF HEARING FROM THE RIGHT PERSON ON E-MAIL ARE BEST IF YOU HOLD OUT FOR A FULL 17 MINUTES...

Panel 11: ...AND, OF COURSE, THE CHANCE OF THE MESSAGE EQUALING YOUR ROMANTIC FANTASY IMPROVES IF YOU TURN YOUR BACK TO THE COMPUTER AND PRETEND TO BE DOING SOMETHING ELSE WHILE IT LOGS ON!!

Panel 12: I CAN'T LISTEN TO THIS!! — TECHNOLOGY IS TOO COMPLEX FOR THE MALE MIND.

Panel 1: LOOK! MY ONLINE SWEETIE E-MAILED A LOVE POEM TO ME! HE E-MAILED A PICTURE OF A ROSE! HE E-MAILED A LIST OF ALL THE THINGS HE ADORES ABOUT ME!

Panel 2: MY HUSBAND PICKED UP A SOCK.

OOH! TELL ME ABOUT IT! TELL ME ALL ABOUT IT!!

Panel 3: REALITY WINS.

VIRTUAL BUMMER.

Panel 4: HOWARD ASKED ME OUT FOR COFFEE, AND I ACCEPTED.

DATE ALERT! DATE ALERT!

Panel 5: MOUSSE THE HAIR! SMACK ON THE MAKEUP! PAINT THE TOENAILS! SQUISH INTO THE MINI! RADIATE THE ATTITUDE!

Panel 6: TRANSFORM YOURSELF INTO SOMEONE EVEN YOU DON'T RECOGNIZE, AND THEN SPEND THE NEXT FIVE YEARS IN THERAPY ASKING WHY YOU ATTRACT MEN WHO DON'T APPRECIATE THE REAL YOU!

Panel 7: NICE TO SEE THAT MARRIAGE HASN'T CHANGED YOU, CHARLENE.

JUST BECAUSE I LEFT THE CHOIR DOESN'T MEAN I CAN'T STILL BELT OUT THE HYMNS.

Panel 8: WHAT ARE YOU GOING TO WEAR TO MEET HOWARD FOR THE FIRST TIME, CATHY?

OH, PLEASE, CHARLENE.

Panel 9: HOWARD AND I HAVE SPENT FIVE HOURS A DAY ONLINE WITH EACH OTHER FOR TWO WEEKS! I KNOW HIM BETTER THAN ANYONE I'VE EVER DATED!

Panel 10: WHAT I WEAR TO MEET A MAN WHO ALREADY COMPLETELY ACCEPTS AND ADORES ME HARDLY MATTERS!

Panel 11: WHAT COUNTS IS WHAT IS HE GOING TO WEAR.

PRECISELY. ONE ICKY GOLF SHIRT, AND THE WHOLE THING COULD BE OFF.

LADIES

BATHROOM:

I LOOK FABULOUS! I FEEL INCREDIBLE!

HALLWAY:

I LOOK VERY NICE. I FEEL PRETTY GOOD.

FRONT DOOR:

I LOOK FINE. I FEEL OK.

OUTSIDE:

I LOOK RIDICULOUS! I FEEL STUPID! WHAT WAS I THINKING??!

CONFIDENCE IS LIKE A CORDLESS PHONE. THE FARTHER FROM THE BASE UNIT, THE WORSE IT FUNCTIONS.

WHAT IF HE'S THE ONE?? DO I WANT TO TELL MY GRANDCHILDREN THAT I MET GRANDPA IN A CLICHÉD COFFEE EMPORIUM??

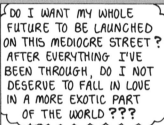

DO I WANT MY WHOLE FUTURE TO BE LAUNCHED ON THIS MEDIOCRE STREET? AFTER EVERYTHING I'VE BEEN THROUGH, DO I NOT DESERVE TO FALL IN LOVE IN A MORE EXOTIC PART OF THE WORLD???

IT'S ALL WRONG! WRONG PLACE! WRONG STREET! WRONG CITY! **IT'S ALL WRONG, WRONG! WRONG!**

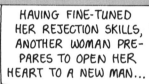

HAVING FINE-TUNED HER REJECTION SKILLS, ANOTHER WOMAN PREPARES TO OPEN HER HEART TO A NEW MAN...

IF YOU TELL ME WHAT YOUR BLIND DATE ALLEGEDLY LOOKS LIKE, MAYBE I CAN HELP YOU SPOT HIM!

IT IS **NOT** A BLIND DATE!

OH. YOU HAD THAT EYEBALL-ING-EVERYONE-WHO-COMES-IN BLIND DATE LOOK ABOUT YOU.

IT IS **NOT** A BLIND DATE!

WE'VE BEEN EMOTIONALLY INVOLVED ONLINE FOR WEEKS! WE JUST HAVEN'T INTERFACED AS OUR VISUAL SELVES YET! IT IS...

...**NOT A BLIND DATE! NOT A BLIND DATE!**

THAT MUST BE HIM NOW.

CURSES ON THE COMPUTER ILLITERATE.

Panel 1: DON'T STARE AT THE FACE. DON'T GAWK AT THE BODY. DON'T LOOK DISAPPOINTED. DON'T APPEAR RELIEVED.

Panel 2: DON'T ACT NERVOUS. DON'T BE ALOOF. DON'T FIDGET. DON'T SWEAT. DON'T GIGGLE. DON'T TWITCH. DON'T BABBLE. DON'T CLUTCH.

Panel 3: DON'T LOOK AT ANYTHING OR DO ANYTHING OR SEEM ANY WAY AT ALL.

Panel 4: IT ISN'T A BLIND DATE. IT'S A BLANK DATE!

Panel 5: SO, CATHY... ...WE FINALLY MEET...
YES...YES, WE FINALLY MEET, HOWARD...

Panel 6: I'VE SPENT FIFTY HOURS TALKING TO YOU ONLINE, AND I CAN'T THINK OF ONE THING TO SAY TO YOU IN PERSON.
ME EITHER. NOTHING. ZILCH.

Panel 7: (no text)

Panel 8: WHAT CAN I BRING YOU?
TWO LAPTOPS WITH MODEMS AND PRE-INSTALLED NET ACCESS SOFTWARE!!

Dear Cathy, Maybe we were too nervous to speak when we met. - H.

Dear Howard, Yes! Just good old-fashioned insecurity. - C.

Dear Cathy, Maybe we should try again. I must see you! - H.

Dear Howard, I must see you too! It will all be different this time! - C.

NOPE.

Dear Cathy, Maybe the location is wrong. - H.

Dear Howard, Sensory overload! Too many airborne caffeine particles...

Dear Cathy, The indoors was too stifling for conversation. Maybe we should try a park. - H.

Dear Howard, Yes! We'll bring our dogs! Our dogs can romp while we interface in the park! - C.

NOPE. NOPE. NOPE. NOPE.

Dear Howard, I only seem to have feelings for you on a screen. - C.

Dear Cathy, The park was too phony! We'll meet in a software store....

HOWARD AND I TRIED MEETING IN A COFFEE SHOP. NO CHEMISTRY. WE MET AT A PARK. NO CHEMISTRY.

WE MET AT A MALL, A BOOKSTORE, A SOFTWARE STORE, A JUICE BAR, A BAKERY, A MUSEUM, A COPY PLACE...

THERE'S NO ATTRACTION. NO CURIOSITY. NO TWINGE. NOTHING. A COMPLETE, MUTUAL, TOTAL LACK OF INTEREST.

SO YOU'RE NOT EVEN GOING TO **TRY**??!!

FUNNY HOW THE MARRIED PEOPLE ARE ALWAYS MORE DESPERATE THAN THE SINGLE PEOPLE.

HOWARD AND I HAVE NO INTEREST IN DATING EACH OTHER. DO I KEEP THE RELATIONSHIP GOING ONLINE OR TELL HIM TO FORGET IT?

WHY GIVE UP A FABULOUS RELATIONSHIP JUST BECAUSE IT ONLY EXISTS ON THE INTERNET?...THEN AGAIN, WHY WASTE MY TIME ON AN ONLINE LOVE THAT WILL NEVER LEAD TO ANYTHING ELSE?

FROM THE HIGH-TECH WORLD OF COMPUTERS, YET ANOTHER EXHILARATING NEW FRONTIER...

...TRYING TO DECIDE WHETHER OR NOT TO BREAK UP WITH A MAN I'M NOT GOING OUT WITH.

A DATE? YOU HAVE ANOTHER DATE WITH HOWARD??

IT'S NOT REALLY A DATE, MOM. WE'RE JUST GETTING TOGETHER TO OFFICIALLY BREAK UP.

YOU'RE GOING OUT TO BREAK UP?

WELL, IT'S NOT REALLY BREAKING UP SINCE WE HAVEN'T TECHNICALLY BEEN DATING.

IT'S MORE A FORMAL EXERCISE WHERE WE VERBALIZE OUR MUTUAL LACK OF INTEREST AND INTENTION TO HAVE NO CONTACT WHATSOEVER IN THE FUTURE.

SO MANY CEREMONIES, SO FEW WEDDINGS.

WE NEVER DID ANYTHING TOGETHER, HOWARD, SO THERE ARE NO POSSESSIONS TO RETURN!

NO PHOTOS TO RIP UP!

NO MEMORIES TO OBLITERATE!

NO KEYS TO EXCHANGE!

THE RELATIONSHIP ONLY EXISTED IN CYBERSPACE! IT WAS JUST TYPING!

JUST TWO WEEKS OF TYPING UNTIL 3:00 AM, AND NOW IT'S OVER!

I WANT THE 56 HOURS OF SLEEP I MISSED BACK!!

HOWARD AND I HAD NOTHING TO TALK ABOUT IN PERSON, MOM.

LOTS OF TIMES YOUR FATHER AND I HAVE NOTHING TO TALK ABOUT, CATHY!

NO. I MEAN WE DIDN'T SPEAK! THERE WAS NOTHING TO SAY!

DAD AND I CAN GO A WHOLE WEEKEND WITHOUT MAKING A PEEP!

MOM, THERE WAS **NOTHING**! NO SPARKS! NO FIRE! **NO CONVERSATION WHATSOEVER**!

HOW GLORIOUS! THE GLORIOUS COMFORT ZONE OF JUST BEING WITH EACH OTHER!

BLEAH.

WHY IS IT THAT WHAT MAKES MARRIAGE WORK, MAKES DATING FAIL....

I SHOULDN'T HAVE HAD THAT FIRST TASTE. NOW I WANT MORE.

NOT A LOT MORE. JUST A LITTLE MORE. IF I HAVE A LITTLE MORE, I'LL BE HAPPY AND I'LL GO RIGHT TO BED...

...OOH, WAIT... NOW I HAVE TO TRY THAT... AND I HAVE TO TRY THAT... AND I HAVE TO TRY THAT...

THE INTERNET: MENTAL EQUIVALENT OF AN OPENED BOX OF CHOCOLATES.

LOOKING FOR A NEW SUIT? NO.

SWIMWEAR

I WAS LURED INTO YOUR DEPARTMENT BY THE SAME INEXPLICABLE FORCE THAT DRAWS PEOPLE TO HORROR MOVIES...A LUST AFTER SOME TERROR SO HIDEOUS THAT, BY COMPARISON, ALL THE REST OF LIFE WILL SEEM MANAGEABLE.

THE STRING BIKINI IS BACK.

AACK!

AT LEAST OUR AUDIENCE NEVER LEAVES DISAPPOINTED.

THE "MY-LIFE-IS-TOO-STRESSFUL-TO-BE-ON-A-DIET-RIGHT-NOW" MUSCLE: TONED AND TRIM.

THE "I-WAS-FORCED-TO-EAT-FETTUCCINI-ALFREDO-AT-A-BUSINESS-LUNCH" MUSCLE: LEAN AND FIT.

THE "I'M-A-VICTIM-OF-A-FLABBY-GENE-POOL" MUSCLE: SCULPTED, SHAPED AND STRONG.

THE "I-HAVE-BETTER-THINGS-TO-DO-WITH-MY-TIME-THAN-BE-TORTURED-IN-SOME-SWEATY-GYM" MUSCLE: HARD AS STEEL.

FROM THE NECK UP, I'M PRACTICALLY AN OLYMPIAN.

38

Panel 1: WHAT THE ENTIRE POPULATION OF THE WORLD SEES:

Panel 2: WHAT THE WOMAN IN THE SWIMSUIT SEES:

Panel 3: ONCE AGAIN, ONE TINY EGO OUTVOTES 5,734,000,000 PEOPLE.

Panel 4: EVER SENSITIVE TO THE NEEDS OF THE SWIMWEAR SHOPPER, WE HAVE COORDINATING COVER-UPS FOR MANY OF THIS YEAR'S SUITS!

THANK HEAVENS.

Panel 5: SEE? TEENSY CROPPED TEE COVER-UPS... STRETCH FABRIC MINI-SHORT COVER-UPS...

THESE WON'T COVER ANYTHING UP!

Panel 6: THESE NOT ONLY MAKE WHAT THEY'RE FAILING TO COVER UP LOOK WORSE, THEY CREATE ENTIRE NEW FOCAL DISASTER POINTS!

Panel 7: FORGET THE COVER-UPS! I LOOK BETTER IN THE GROSS SUIT THAN I DO IN THE REPULSIVE COVER-UPS!!

SWIMWEAR, 1996: A WHOLE NEW KIND OF CONFIDENCE.

Panel 8: DARK GLASSES. CHECK.
HUGE FLOPPY HAT. CHECK.
GIANT TOWEL. CHECK.
UPLIFTING MUSIC. CHECK.

3

Panel 9: WHY DID YOU MAKE US PACK THE SAME THINGS TO TRY ON BATHING SUITS THAT WE USED TO PACK TO WEAR THE BATHING SUITS, CATHY?

TURN AND FACE THE MIRROR, CHARLENE.

Panel 10:

Panel 11: CELLULAR PHONE PRE-DIALED TO THERAPIST'S PHONE NUMBER.

CHECK.

WHY CAN'T WOMEN WEAR BAGGY TRUNKS AND T-SHIRTS TO SWIM IN LIKE MEN DO?

DON'T BE RIDICULOUS.

TUMMY CONTROL

WHY NOT? IT'S A UNISEX WORLD! UNISEX JEANS... UNISEX SWEATSUITS... EVEN UNISEX COLOGNE!

WHY NOT UNISEX SWIMWEAR? WHY NOT LET WOMEN BE AS COMFORTABLE AT THE POOL AS MEN FOR ONCE IN LIFE??!

IT JUST ISN'T DONE.

FORGET DRESS-DOWN FRIDAY. WHAT WE NEED IS DRESS-DOWN SATURDAY AFTERNOON.

TUMMY CONTROL

WOMEN OUR AGE HAVE FOUGHT FOR TWENTY YEARS TO NOT BE VIEWED AS SEX OBJECTS.

BIKINI

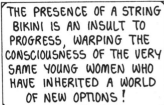

THE PRESENCE OF A STRING BIKINI IS AN INSULT TO PROGRESS, WARPING THE CONSCIOUSNESS OF THE VERY SAME YOUNG WOMEN WHO HAVE INHERITED A WORLD OF NEW OPTIONS!

SAY NO, YOUNG WOMEN! REJECT THE BIKINI AND EMBRACE THE EMANCI-PATION!!

IF YOU HAD THAT BODY, YOU WOULDN'T WEAR ONE??

BIKINI

WHERE SOLIDARITY LEAVES OFF, FLABIDARITY BEGINS.

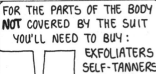
HOW CAN YOU CHARGE $95 FOR THIS PUNY SWIMSUIT??!

SIMPLE.

SWIM

FOR THE PARTS OF THE BODY NOT COVERED BY THE SUIT YOU'LL NEED TO BUY:

EXFOLIATERS
SELF-TANNERS
THIGH CREMES
LOOFAHS
BODY BRUSHES
POLISHERS
WAXERS
BLEACHERS
SHAVERS
SUN SCREENS
AND EXERCISE
EQUIPMENT.

WHEN YOU ADD UP WHAT YOU SPEND DISGUISING THE REST OF THE BODY, THE SWIM-SUIT IS PRACTICALLY FREE!

OH.

WHERE COMPARISON SHOPPING LEAVES OFF, COMPARISON SELLING BEGINS.

SWIM

I READ "THE T-FACTOR DIET" AND WAS CONVINCED THE KEY TO WEIGHT LOSS IS EATING LOW-FAT COMPLEX CARBOHYDRATES.

I READ "THE ZONE" AND WAS CONVINCED THE KEY TO WEIGHT LOSS IS EATING PROTEIN AND MONO-UNSATURATED FAT.

I READ "WHY WOMEN NEED CHOCOLATE" AND WAS CONVINCED THE KEY TO WEIGHT LOSS IS EATING WHAT THE BODY NATURALLY CRAVES.

IT ISN'T FAT. IT'S INFORMATION OVERLOAD.

HERE ARE MY VACATION PHONE NUMBERS IN CASE YOU HEAR ANY RUMORS ABOUT "DOWNSIZING" THAT COULD AFFECT MY JOB WHILE I'M GONE!

HERE'S MY RESORT FAX NUMBER IN CASE YOU SENSE ANY "RESTRUCTURING" THAT COULD IMPACT MY SALARY WHILE I'M GONE!

HERE'S MY BEEPER CODE AND E-MAIL ADDRESS IN CASE YOU HEAR ONE PEEP ABOUT "CUTBACKS" WHILE I'M GONE!

MOST POPULAR VACATION DESTINATION OF 1996: PARANOIA-VILLE.

HI, CATHY. HAS ANYTHING HAPPENED?

YOU JUST LEFT ON VACATION YESTERDAY, FRED.

ANY SUSPICIOUS MEMOS ABOUT COST CONTROL?? ANY YOUNG STRANGERS IN THE OFFICE WHO LOOK LIKE THEY'D DO MY JOB FOR $18,000 A YEAR??!

...OH, I GET IT! YOU CAN'T TALK! THE BOSS IS THERE, ISN'T HE?....OR ARE YOU AFTER MY JOB, TOO?? NO WONDER YOU'RE NOT ON VACATION THIS WEEK! I'M ON SPEAKER PHONE, AREN'T I?? AACK! HI, EVERYONE! HA, HA, JUST KIDDING....

IT'S FINALLY HAPPENED. IT'S LESS STRESSFUL TO BE HERE THAN TO BE ON VACATION FROM HERE.

RECEPTION

YOU HAVE NO SOCCER TEAM TO PLAN YOUR VACATION AROUND, CATHY... NO DAY CAMP TO FIT IN...NO MUSIC LESSONS TO COORDINATE... NO DUAL-CAREER SCHEDULES TO CONSIDER.....

YOU HAVE NO CONFLICTS! NO RESTRICTIONS! NO LIMITATIONS!

I ALSO HAVE NO PLANS.

AH. THE PARALYSIS OF FREE-DOM. IT'S STARTING TO COME BACK...

I CAN'T BOOK TICKETS! I HAVEN'T MET MY HYPOTHE-TICAL TRAV-ELING COM-PANION YET!

43

YOU CAN'T PLAN A VACATION WITHOUT VISITING THE TRAVEL WEB SITES, CATHY! YOU CAN EVEN BOOK YOUR PLANE ON...

THAT DOES IT.

CAN'T ANYONE DO ANYTHING ANYMORE WITHOUT INVOLVING THE WORLD WIDE WEB?? MUST EVERY TASK NOW INCLUDE 2,000 WEB SITES I DON'T HAVE TIME TO LOOK UP?

IF I'M GOING TO TAKE A VACATION, IT WILL BE TO SOMEWHERE WHERE THEY'VE NEVER HEARD OF THE INTERNET!!

TRY PLUTO.

NO GOOD. THAT'S WHERE ALL THE MEN ARE. AN ONLINE SERVICE IS PUMPED IN WITH THE OXYGEN SUPPLY.

EVERYONE HAS FABULOUS VACATION PLANS EXCEPT ME, MOM!...SOME GRAND CONCEPT...SOME BIG ADVENTURE...SOME GREAT RATE...

I HAVE **NOTHING**! NO PLACE TO GO, NO ONE TO GO WITH... **NOTHING**!

YOUR FATHER AND I ARE TAKING A NICE, SCENIC, FOUR-DAY DRIVE ACROSS THE STATE TO VISIT AUNT RUTH. YOU AND ELECTRA CAN COME ALONG IN THE BACK SEAT!

OOPS! GOTTA GO, MOM! TRAVEL AGENT ON LINE TWO!

SOME PARENTS GIVE THEIR CHILDREN WINGS. I JUST GAVE OURS A TURBO JET.

A DOG? OH, NO. THIS IS A NICE HOTEL. NO DOGS.

WHY NOT?

IT'S **PEOPLE** WHO STEAL THINGS, BREAK THINGS AND SPILL THINGS! **PEOPLE** BURN THINGS, RIP THINGS, DRAW ON THINGS, JUMP ON THINGS AND SLOBBER ON THINGS!

PEOPLE HAVE LOUD, SCREAMING PARTIES, AND WHEN THEY'RE CAUGHT DOING ANY OF IT, PEOPLE DON'T EVEN GET THAT SWEET, FORLORN LOOK ON THEIR FACES!

I KNOW WHY WE DON'T ALLOW DOGS. WHY EXACTLY DO WE ALLOW THE HUMANS?

Reservations

44

YOU'RE VACATIONING AT HOME, ANDREA? WHAT WILL YOU DO AT HOME ALL WEEK?

ARE YOU KIDDING??

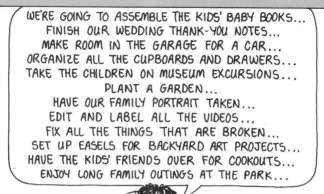

WE'RE GOING TO ASSEMBLE THE KIDS' BABY BOOKS...
FINISH OUR WEDDING THANK-YOU NOTES...
MAKE ROOM IN THE GARAGE FOR A CAR...
ORGANIZE ALL THE CUPBOARDS AND DRAWERS...
TAKE THE CHILDREN ON MUSEUM EXCURSIONS...
PLANT A GARDEN...
HAVE OUR FAMILY PORTRAIT TAKEN...
EDIT AND LABEL ALL THE VIDEOS...
FIX ALL THE THINGS THAT ARE BROKEN...
SET UP EASELS FOR BACKYARD ART PROJECTS...
HAVE THE KIDS' FRIENDS OVER FOR COOKOUTS...
ENJOY LONG FAMILY OUTINGS AT THE PARK...

TO DO ON VACATION

WHY NOT GO AWAY SOMEWHERE?

WE DON'T WANT THE STRESS AND PRESSURE OF TRAVEL.

MOM?

YES, ZENITH! I'M HERE FOR YOU!

MOMMY'S USUALLY SO BUSY WORKING AND DOING ERRANDS AND TRYING TO KEEP THE HOUSE TOGETHER... BUT I'M ON VACATION NOW! I'M ALL YOURS, AND WE CAN TALK ABOUT EVERYTHING IN THE WORLD YOU WANT TO TALK ABOUT!

WHY AREN'T WE COMPOSTING OUR BIODEGRADABLE TRASH?

LUKE??!!

I HAVE TO RUN OVER TO THE OFFICE FOR A FEW MINUTES.

STAMP PAINTING!

WHY NOT?

LET'S JUST LEAVE THE FIRST GIANT MESS AND GET OUT ANOTHER GIANT MESS!

LET'S GET OUT ALL THE TOYS AND MIX UP ALL THE PIECES AND THEN PLOP DOWN IN THE MIDDLE OF IT AND EAT ICE CREAM AND WATCH TV!!

...HONEY??

I FOUND MY INNER CHILD, BUT I CAN NO LONGER LOCATE MY INNER GROWN-UP.

FROOT LOOP RUSH. WANT SOME, DAD?

45

...THIS IS LIFE AS IT SHOULD BE! MOMMY, DADDY, ZENITH AND GUS ON A LOVELY FAMILY PICNIC!

BONK!
WAAAH!!
RIP RIP
SPLOOSH!
STOMP STOMP STOMP
SHRED
SPLAT
CLUNK!
RIP RIP
BONK!

NOTICE THEY CALL THEM "PRECIOUS MOMENTS," NOT "PRECIOUS MINUTES," ANDREA.

I WAS SHOOTING FOR A PRECIOUS HALF-HOUR.

WE'RE IN THE KITCHEN, MOM!

I'M COMING! JUST LET ME CARRY IN THE DISHES AND BOTTLES AND PAPERS FROM THE LIVING ROOM!

WE'RE IN OUR ROOM, MOM!

OK, SWEETIE! I JUST HAVE TO GRAB THE CLEAN CLOTHES AND SHEETS AND TOYS FROM THE KITCHEN!

WE'RE IN THE LIVING ROOM!

COMING! JUST LET ME BRING THE MARKERS AND BLOCKS FROM YOUR ROOM AND SOME LEMONADE AND A LITTLE SNACK!

VACATIONERS PACK TO TRAVEL TO DISTANT LANDS. MOTHERS PACK TO GET FROM ONE ROOM TO ANOTHER.

PEANUT BUTTER

..."BUCK" IS WHAT?..HIS BLUE TRUCK??...OH, YES! OF COURSE! I KNEW THAT! HA, HA! SILLY ME...

I HAD TO CALL A STRANGER TO FIND OUT WHAT MY SON WAS ASKING FOR, LUKE!!

GUS IS IN DAY CARE ALL WEEK, ANDREA. YOU CAN'T KNOW EVERYTHING.

SOMEONE KNOWS HIM BETTER THAN I DO! SHE'S TEACHING HIM SONGS I'VE NEVER HEARD...READING HIM BOOKS I'VE NEVER....

BUBOO, MAMA, BUBOO!

"LOVE YOU"?? GUS SAID "I LOVE YOU"!!

"BUBOO" IS WHAT HE CALLS HIS X-MAN SIPPY CUP.

LET'S LET HER HAVE THIS ONE, HONEY.

46

SIMON AND I ARE SPENDING OUR VACATION PLANNING OUR RETURN TO THE SIMPLE LIFE!

THE SIMPLE LIFE?

SEE? IT'S ALL RIGHT HERE ON OUR NEW LAPTOP! WE'RE PLEDGING TO GET OFF THE FAST TRACK AND REDISCOVER THE SIMPLE, HEALTHY, STRESS-FREE PLEASURES OF LIFE!

YOU NEED A COMPUTER FOR THAT?

OH, YES. WE NEED THE COMPUTER, PRINTER AND MODEM... ...AND, OF COURSE, WE NEED THE PHONES, FAX, VCR, CAMCORDER, JUICER, ESPRESSO MACHINE, FOOD PROCESSOR, TWO CARS, MICROWAVE, PLAQUE REMOVER AND HOME GYM....

SO FAR, THE ONLY THINGS WE'RE SURE WE WANT TO GET RID OF ARE OUR JOBS.

SHOULD I LEAVE MY DESK MESSY SO IT LOOKS AS IF I'M BUSY AND CRUCIAL TO THE COMPANY... OR SHOULD I LEAVE IT NEAT SO IT LOOKS AS IF I'M PROFESSIONAL AND ORGANIZED?

IF I LEAVE IT MESSY, NO ONE WILL BE ABLE TO FIND ANYTHING WHEN I'M ON VACATION, AND WILL THAT MAKE ME SEEM MORE OR LESS IMPORTANT?

IF I LEAVE IT NEAT, WILL I BE SNEERED AT FOR BEING COMPULSIVE, OR ADMIRED FOR BEING CONSIDERATE?

FIFTY MAGAZINE ARTICLES ON HOW TO PACK, AND NOTHING ON HOW TO ARRANGE WHAT I LEAVE BEHIND.

HOW ARE WE DOING, CATHY?

HALF OF THOSE ON VACATION ARE PANICKED THAT THEY WON'T HAVE JOBS WHEN THEY GET BACK...

...AND THE OTHER HALF ARE SICK OF SACRIFICING THEIR LIVES TO A BUSINESS THAT COULD CRUMBLE ANYWAY, AND ARE SPENDING THEIR VACATIONS TRYING TO FIGURE OUT HOW THEY CAN QUIT.

NO, NOT OUR WHINERS... OUR CLIENTS! HOW ARE WE DOING WITH OUR CLIENTS?!

THOSE ARE OUR CLIENTS, MR. PINKLEY.

WHEN I DREAMED OF THE DAY WE'D ALL BE IN SYNC, I WASN'T THINKING HOW CLOSE WE'D BE TO THE DRAIN.

I'M SICK OF MY "HEALTHY FOOD PROGRAM FOR LIFE"!! I WANT RESULTS!!

ARE YOU LIMITING YOUR FAT INTAKE? YES.

ARE YOU CONTROLLING PORTION SIZE? YES.

ARE YOU SLOWLY LEARNING TO THINK OF FOOD AS NUTRITION, NOT THERAPY? YES.

YOU **HAVE** RESULTS, CATHY! YOU'RE MAKING REAL HEADWAY!

I'M SICK OF HEADWAY! I WANT TO MAKE REARWAY!

THE SCARSDALE DIET? NO. 1990s FAT IS TOO HEALTH-SAVVY TO RESPOND TO SOME 1970s FAD.

YOU THINK YOUR FAT KNOWS THAT SCARSDALE WAS A '70s FAD??

MY FAT LIVES HERE IN THE SAME HOUSE WITH EVERYONE ELSE. YOU THINK IT DOESN'T HEAR?

EVEN IF IT DIDN'T HEAR DIRECTLY, MY CURRENT FAT IS JUST A DESCENDANT OF PREVIOUS FAT WHO RAISED IT ON HORROR STORIES OF CARBOHYDRATE DEPRIVATION.

AH, THE POWER OF THE MIND-BODY CONNECTION...

WHO HAS A PAMPHLET ON FEN-PHEN? MY THIGHS CRAVE INNOVATION!!

QUICK! I NEED TO LOSE FIVE POUNDS IN THE NEXT FOUR DAYS!

I THOUGHT YOU WERE GOING TO GET THE NEW DIET DRUG FROM YOUR DOCTOR, CATHY.

I AM! MY APPOINTMENT'S IN FOUR DAYS! HE CAN'T SEE ME LIKE THIS!

I HAVE TO AT LEAST GET MYSELF BACK TO THE CONDITION I WAS IN THE LAST TIME HE SAW ME! QUICK! EMERGENCY! EMERGENCY!!

THE "CLEANING-THE-HOUSE-BEFORE-THE-CLEANING-PERSON-COMES" APPROACH TO DIETING.

I'D HATE FOR MY DIET DOCTOR TO THINK I'M OVERWEIGHT.

YOU LOST FOUR POUNDS OVER THE WEEKEND ON ATKINS?! AACK! I SHOULD HAVE DONE ATKINS!

YOU LOST FIVE POUNDS ON THE "FIVE-DAY MIRACLE DIET" ?? NO! WHY DIDN'T I DO THE "FIVE-DAY MIRACLE DIET" ?!

YOU LOST SIX POUNDS ON CABBAGE SOUP? I COULD HAVE DONE CABBAGE SOUP! I COULD HAVE DONE LIQUID PROTEIN!...WHY DIDN'T I LISTEN TO THE FALSE CLAIMS? WHY? WHY?!!

THERE, THERE, CATHY...

HOW MANY TEARS MUST I SHED BEFORE I LOSE A POUND OF WATER WEIGHT?

YOU WANT THE DIET DRUG? WELL, I'M NOT GOING TO SAY ANYTHING, CATHY.

GOOD, MOM.

IF I SAY SOMETHING, YOU'LL BE MORE INCLINED TO DO THE OPPOSITE, SO I WON'T SAY ANYTHING AT ALL.

GOOD.

YOU DIDN'T ASK FOR MY OPINION, SO I'M NOT GIVING MY OPINION. I'LL JUST SIT HERE IN UTTER SILENCE, HOPING AND PRAYING YOU DO THE RIGHT THING!

INCREDIBLE HOW MANY WORDS CAN COME OUT OF LIPS THAT ARE SEALED.

YOU CANCELED YOUR DOCTOR APPOINTMENT, CATHY??

I DECIDED TO WAIT AND SEE IF MARCIA LOSES WEIGHT ON THE DIET DRUG BEFORE I TRY IT.

JUST TRY IT! EVERYONE SAYS IT'S FABULOUS!

I DON'T KNOW EVERYONE. I KNOW MARCIA.

BUT I DON'T KNOW MARCIA! I WANT YOU TO TRY IT SO IF IT WORKS ON YOU I CAN TRY IT!

I'M NOT TRYING IT UNTIL I SEE HOW IT WORKS ON MARCIA!

WE WAITED YEARS FOR F.D.A. APPROVAL. NOW WE'RE WAITING FOR MARCIA TO WEIGH IN.

Panel 1:
- LOW-SODIUM, FAT-FREE, HIGH-BULK BRAN MUFFIN?
- NO! IT'S 10:30. TIME FOR MY HARD-CHEW SNACK!
- I NEED A HORMONE-BALANCING PROTEIN INFUSION!
- CABBAGE SOUP! MOVE OVER SO I CAN HEAT MY CABBAGE SOUP!

Panel 2:
- BLEAH! YOU'RE MAKING ME SICK! LET ME OUT OF HERE! **BLEAH!!**

Panel 3:
- NO INDIVIDUAL PROGRESS, BUT AS A GROUP, WE LOST 190 POUNDS IN 14 SECONDS.

Panel 4:
- I'VE PUT UP THE MENTAL BARRICADES... SEALED THE EMOTIONAL WINDOWS... ...SPRAYED ANXIETY REPELLENT ALL OVER THE PLACE... ..AND YET I FEEL IT COMING...

Panel 5:
- AS PREDICTABLE AND UNRELENTING AND FORMIDABLE AND UNSTOPPABLE AS THE INVASION OF THE SUMMER ANTS...
- RING RING

Panel 6:
- WAAH!!
- HI, MOM.

Panel 7:
- ...WELCOME TO WEDDING SEASON.

Panel 8:
- INVITATION TO WEDDING OF LAST SINGLE GIRLFRIEND.
- INVITATION TO WEDDING OF EX-BOYFRIEND.
- INVITATION TO WEDDING OF GIRL I USED TO BABY-SIT.
- Triple Fudge

Panel 9:
- THE MONTH OF JULY: INVITATION TO DIET DISASTER.
- Triple Fudge

Panel 1: ANOTHER ONE? / CLAUDIA.

Panel 2: "Dear Friends, / After twenty years of watching my best friends snatch up all the decent single men... ...throwing $500 bridal showers for them... ...buying $300 bridesmaid dresses...and shelling out $150 a pop for gifts, I, Claudia, am pleased to invite you to celebrate my marriage to Brian. Toll-free number of Tiffany's Catalog enclosed."

Panel 3: THE NEW TRADITIONALIST. / MARRY FOR LOVE AND HAVE THE WEDDING FOR REVENGE.

Panel 4: I CAN'T LET YOU LIVE LIKE THIS ANYMORE, CATHY! OUT WITH THE OVER-ROMANTICIZED NOTIONS! OUT WITH THE IMPRACTICAL DREAMS! OUT WITH THE GRAND ILLUSIONS!

Panel 5: ...OF COURSE, OVER-ROMANTICIZED NOTIONS, IMPRACTICAL DREAMS AND GRAND ILLUSIONS KEEP YOUR HEART ALIVE AND WILL HELP KEEP THE FIRE IN WHATEVER RELATIONSHIP YOU WIND UP IN...

Panel 6: ...SO KEEP EVERYTHING! JUST SQUASH IT ALL OVER TO ONE SIDE AND MAKE SPACE FOR SOMEONE NEW IN THERE!!

Panel 7: MOTHER'S TRYING TO CLEAN OUT MY EMOTIONAL CLOSET. / WE NEED MENTAL STORAGE BINS, AND WE NEED THEM NOW!

Panel 8: I HAVE NO INTEREST IN FLO'S NEPHEW, MOM. / YOU DON'T HAVE TO MARRY HIM, CATHY. YOU CAN JUST BE FRIENDS.

Panel 9: IF HE'S INTERESTED IN ME AND I'M NOT INTERESTED IN HIM, WE'RE NOT GOING TO BE FRIENDS... IF I'M INTERESTED IN HIM AND HE'S NOT INTERESTED IN ME, WE'RE NOT GOING TO BE FRIENDS...

Panel 10: THE ONLY WAY A MAN AND WOMAN CAN BE GENUINE FRIENDS IS IF THEY'RE MUTUALLY REPULSED BY EACH OTHER AND JUST CALL NOW AND THEN WHEN THEY'RE DESPERATE TO MAKE SURE NOTHING'S CHANGED!!

Panel 11: PHONE FRIENDS! IT'S A START! / BEHIND EVERY CLOUD IS A SILVER LINING AND A MOTHER CLUTCHING A LITTLE JAR OF SILVER POLISH.

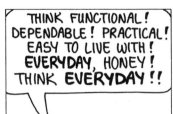

Panel 1: WOULDN'T THIS BE NICE FOR... / SHOWY BUT IMPRACTICAL! GORGEOUS BUT DANGEROUS TO TOUCH!

Bridal Registry

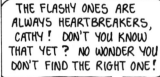

Panel 2: THE FLASHY ONES ARE ALWAYS HEARTBREAKERS, CATHY! DON'T YOU KNOW THAT YET? NO WONDER YOU DON'T FIND THE RIGHT ONE!

Bridal Registry

Panel 3: THINK FUNCTIONAL! DEPENDABLE! PRACTICAL! EASY TO LIVE WITH! **EVERYDAY**, HONEY! THINK **EVERYDAY**!!

Panel 4: ARE WE SHOPPING FOR A GIFT OR FOR A GROOM? / WHY? DO YOU KNOW SOMEONE?

Bridal Registry

Panel 5: I HAVE FOUR WEDDINGS TO GO TO BY THE END OF SUMMER! / WE HAVE FOUR ACRES OF WOOL!

FALL · TWEED · VELVET · WOOL PANT

Panel 6: ONE WEDDING IS FORMAL, ONE GARDEN, ONE EVENING, ONE CASUAL. / ONE RACK IS TWEEDS, ONE IS VELVETS, ONE IS COATS, ONE IS SWEATERS!

FALL · TWE

Panel 7: I WANT BREEZY STRAW HATS AND ACCESSORIES FOR ALL! / BROWN FEDORAS AND 20,000 BOOTS!

Panel 8: SUMMER MEETS FALL, KNOWS IT'S DOOMED, BUT TRIES TO STRIKE UP A ROMANCE ANYWAY.

WHERE DO WE START? / RIGHT THIS WAY...

FALL · TWEED · VELVET · WOOL PANT

Panel 9: DID YOU FIND SOMETHING FOR ADRIENNE'S WEDDING, CATHY? / TA DA! NEW SUEDE BOOTS TO QUIET MY JEALOUS WHINING...

Boots · RECEPTION

Panel 10: ...KICKY NEW PUMPS TO SQUELCH ANY BITTERNESS THAT MAY HAVE CREPT INTO MY VOICE...AND THREE STUNNING NEW PAIRS OF FALL FLATS TO STIFLE ANY RESIDUAL BAD VIBE I MAY HAVE BEEN INCLINED TO EMIT!

Shoes

Panel 11: I SPENT SO MUCH ON FOOTWEAR TODAY THAT I WILL EXUDE ONLY JOY AND LOVE ABOUT ADRIENNE'S UPCOMING MARRIAGE!

Panel 12: THAT'S MY GIRL! / SOME PEOPLE SAY IT WITH FLOWERS. I KEEP IT SILENT WITH SHOES.

Shoes · Boots · Shoes · RECEPTION · Shoes

YAP YAP YAP!

I'M NOT LISTENING TO YOU BECAUSE I'M NOT WAKING UP, ELECTRA!

YAP YAP YAP!

I'M NOT WAKING UP BECAUSE IT'S SATURDAY AND THE LONGER I SLEEP, THE FEWER HOURS OF WILLPOWER I NEED!

AS LONG AS I'M SLEEPING, I'M SAFE FROM FOOD! SAFE FROM TEMPTATION! SAFE FROM....

AP YAP YAP YAP YAP YAP YAP YAP YAP

...GUARD DOG, INDEED...

muffins

ELECTRA

THERE'S A FUN-SOUNDING SINGLES' MIXER ADVERTISED IN THE PAPER, CATHY.

I'M TOO OLD TO GO TO SOME SINGLES' MIXER, MOM.

NONSENSE. MEN LIKE MATURE, DISCRIMINATING WOMEN.

I'M TOO OLD AND TOO PICKY!

I'M NOT MATURE AND DISCRIMINATING.

I'M OLD AND PICKY AND PROUD THAT I'VE REACHED A PLACE IN LIFE WHERE I CAN REJECT WHOLE MIXERS-FULL OF MEN WITHOUT EVEN LEAVING MY BACK PORCH!

YOU NEVER KNOW UNTIL YOU TRY.

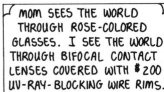

MOM SEES THE WORLD THROUGH ROSE-COLORED GLASSES. I SEE THE WORLD THROUGH BIFOCAL CONTACT LENSES COVERED WITH $200 UV-RAY-BLOCKING WIRE RIMS.

TO JOAN, WHO'S TAKING A THREE-MONTH SABBATICAL TO "REJUVENATE HERSELF IN ITALY"!

TO ELLEN, WHO DUMPED SIX CRISES ON MY DESK ON HER WAY TO FRANCE!

TO KIM, WHO BECAME PREGNANT WITH HER SECOND CHILD ON A CARIBBEAN CRUISE!

TO MARTHA, WHO SENT A POSTCARD SAYING HER BOYFRIEND PROPOSED ON A YACHT IN GREECE!

MAKES YOU KIND OF WONDER, DOESN'T IT?

YEAH...

HOW MANY CALORIES PER SOUR GRAPE?

I LET GO OF MY ANXIETIES! GOT RID OF MY INSECURITIES! DISCARDED SELF-DOUBT!

UNLOADED PAST GARBAGE! THREW OUT MY EMOTIONAL BAGGAGE AND DUMPED MY PERSONAL DEMONS!

THEN I ATE A PIE.

I WAS FEELING SO EMPTY ALL OF A SUDDEN.

JANUARY

WHAT DID YOU DO LAST WEEKEND?

NOTHING.

APRIL

WHAT DID YOU DO LAST NIGHT?

NOTHING.

SEPTEMBER

WHAT DID YOU DO ON YOUR VACATION?

NOTHING! FOR SEVEN GLORIOUS DAYS I DID ABSOLUTELY NOTHING!!

AMAZING HOW MUCH RICHER NOTHING IS WHEN YOU FLY SOMEWHERE TO GET TO IT.

"LIVING THE SIMPLE LIFE" "SIMPLE ABUNDANCE" "VOLUNTARY SIMPLICITY" "SIMPLIFY YOUR LIFE"

EXHAUSTED, DISGUSTED, BROKE AND FRIED, A NATION DESPERATE FOR INNER PEACE LOOKS DEEP WITHIN THE COVERS OF THE BEST SELLERS AND REDISCOVERS THE BASICS....

BEST SELLERS

...JEALOUSY, JEALOUSY AND JEALOUSY.

WHY DIDN'T I WRITE THIS STUPID BOOK AND MAKE A ZILLION DOLLARS?!!

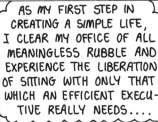
Panel 1: OLD FILES...OUT! OLD MEMOS...OUT! OLD MEETING NOTES...OUT!

Panel 2: AS MY FIRST STEP IN CREATING A SIMPLE LIFE, I CLEAR MY OFFICE OF ALL MEANINGLESS RUBBLE AND EXPERIENCE THE LIBERATION OF SITTING WITH ONLY THAT WHICH AN EFFICIENT EXECUTIVE REALLY NEEDS....

Panel 3: WHERE'S THE KLINE FILE? WHERE'S THE FINN MEMO? WHERE'S THE BARTLY MEETING DOCUMENTATION?

Panel 4: ...NOSE PLUGS AND A PAIR OF RUBBER GLOVES

THERE! I THINK I SEE PART OF THE BATES CONTRACT UNDER THE BURRITO SAUCE....

DUMPSTER

Panel 5: I CAN'T SIMPLIFY MY WARDROBE BECAUSE I NEED THE FULL SPECTRUM OF OUTFITS IN CASE I MEET SOMEONE...

Panel 6: I CAN'T SIMPLIFY MY BATHROOM BECAUSE I NEED IMMEDIATE ACCESS TO ALL BEAUTY PRODUCTS IN CASE I MEET SOMEONE...

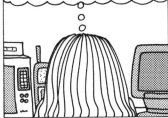
Panel 7: I CAN'T SIMPLIFY MY LIFE BY DISCONNECTING MY ANSWERING MACHINE, PHONE, CABLE OR ONLINE SERVICE BECAUSE UNTIL I MEET THE PERSON, I NEED ALL LINES OF COMMUNICATION OPEN.

Panel 8: SINGLENESS IN THE '90s: DOOMED TO BE OVER-PACKAGED UNTIL WE INSPIRE BRAND LOYALTY.

Panel 9: EVERY ITEM HAS TWO BIG THRILLS: THE THRILL OF BUYING IT, AND THE THRILL OF GETTING RID OF IT.

Panel 10: SOME WOULD QUESTION THE VALUE OF BUYING IT IF GETTING RID OF IT IS SUCH A THRILL.

THE SIMPLE LIFE

Panel 11: I SAY THE GETTING RID OF IT THRILL IS ONLY POSSIBLE BECAUSE OF THE BUYING IT THRILL... THAT TO EXPERIENCE THE FULL THRILLING SPECTRUM OF LIFE, ONE MUST **PURCHASE** THE GARBAGE BEFORE ONE **DUMPS** THE GARBAGE!

Panel 12: THEREFORE, OFF TO THE MALL!

EVERY VISIT HAS TWO BIG THRILLS: THE THRILL WHEN COMPANY COMES, AND THE THRILL WHEN COMPANY GOES AWAY.

Panel 1: ADRIENNE AND GREG ARE GETTING MARRIED IN FOUR HOURS AND I CAN'T GET INTO MY SKIRT, MOM!!

Panel 2: WHY ARE YOU YELLING AT ME, SWEETIE? BECAUSE WHEN YOU REALLY NEED TO LOOK NICE, YOU CAN'T GET INTO YOUR SKIRT... ...GRANDMA COULDN'T GET INTO HER SKIRT... ...GREAT GRANDMA COULDN'T GET INTO HER SKIRT....

Panel 3: EVERY TIME A WOMAN IN OUR FAMILY HAS SOMEWHERE SPECIAL TO GO, SHE CAN'T GET INTO HER SKIRT!

Panel 4: SOME FAMILIES HAVE A LEGACY. WE HAVE A HIP-ACY.

Panel 5: GLANCED AT 33 ARTICLES ON HOW MY GENERATION IS SAVING ONLY A THIRD OF WHAT WE'LL NEED FOR RETIREMENT.... BOUGHT A $300 "WIZARD" WITH AN EXPENSE REPORT FUNCTION.

Panel 6: SAW 12 SPECIAL REPORTS ON HOW THE ONLY PEOPLE WITH JOB SECURITY ARE THOSE WHO STAY ON THE CUTTING EDGE OF TECHNOLOGY ..... BOUGHT A "FAR SIDE" SCREEN SAVER.

Panel 7: SKIMMED FOUR BOOKS ON THE NATIONWIDE TREND TOWARD DOWNSIZING AND SIMPLIFICATION.... BOUGHT "CALVIN KLEIN" SNEAKERS, "ANNE KLEIN" SHADES, A "DKNY" BACKPACK AND A CUP OF "STARBUCKS" SPECIAL BLEND.

Panel 8: THE BABY BOOMER MOTTO: IGNORE THE SIGNS, EMBRACE THE LOGOS.

Panel 9: TOO SUMMERY. TOO WINTERY. TOO SPRINGY. TOO FALL-Y.

Panel 10: TOO SUMMERY. TOO WINTERY. TOO SPRINGY. TOO FALL-Y.

Panel 11: TOO SUMMERY. TOO WINTERY. TOO SPRINGY. TOO FALL-Y.

Panel 12: I AM A WOMAN FOR ALL SEASONS, NONE OF WHICH OCCURS DURING THE SECOND WEEK OF SEPTEMBER.

YOU ARE OLD AND BORING AND UGLY.

YOU WERE A MISTAKE! YOU WERE A FANTASY! YOU WERE A HALLUCINATION! YOU ARE NOT WORTHY OF ME!!

I HAVE ELEGANCE WITHIN! I HAVE CHARISMA AND STYLE! I'M FINISHED WITH YOU!! FINISHED WITH ALL OF YOU!!

ANOTHER WOMAN STANDS POISED TO CONQUER THE WORLD IN HER 13-YEAR-OLD BATHROBE.

THERE ARE TWO WORDS TO DESCRIBE FALL FASHION: LONG AND LEAN.

LONG AND LEAN JACKETS! LONG AND LEAN PANTS! LONG AND LEAN SKIRTS! LONG AND LEAN COATS!

THERE ARE TWO WORDS TO DESCRIBE THE AVERAGE FEMALE SHOPPER: SHORT AND SQUATTY.

IT'S GOING TO BE A LONG WINTER.

AND EXTREMELY LEAN.

FOR WOMEN WHO ARE SICK OF TEETERING AROUND IN CHOPPY LITTLE SUITS AND TOE-CRUSHING PUMPS, FALL FASHION IS ALL **GOOD NEWS!!**

SHOES ARE LOW AND CHUNKY, AND EVERY PIECE OF CLOTHING HAS BEEN REPROPORTIONED FOR A LONG, LEAN, SLEEK, SINEWY LOOK!

IN OTHER WORDS, GOODBYE, STILETTO HEEL! HELLO, STILETTO BODY!

FALL '96

FOR EVEN BETTER NEWS, A FUDGE SHOP JUST OPENED IN THE FOOD COURT.

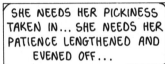

| BATHROOM: | BEDROOM: | OUTSIDE THE FRONT DOOR: | NATURE IN REVERSE: |

 DINNER WITH SOMEONE NEW! WHY NOT? WHAT FUN! HA, HA!

 I LOOK FABULOUS! I FEEL INCREDIBLE! I AM STUNNING!!

 AM I OUT OF MY MIND?! I DON'T EVEN **KNOW** THIS PERSON! I DON'T **WANT** TO KNOW THIS PERSON! BLEAH ON THIS PERSON! BLEAH ON ALL PEOPLE!!

 I'M A BUTTERFLY INSIDE THE COCOON, AND A CATERPILLAR AS SOON AS I COME OUT.

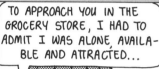 TO APPROACH YOU IN THE GROCERY STORE, I HAD TO ADMIT I WAS ALONE, AVAILABLE AND ATTRACTED...

 IN ONE SPLIT SECOND, I HAD TO MAKE PEACE WITH FIFTEEN YEARS OF FAILED RELATIONSHIPS... DROP MY SHELL... SMASH THROUGH MY DEFENSES... WRENCH OPEN MY SOUL... ...AND LAY MY EGO OUT TO BE TRAMPLED BY A COMPLETE STRANGER LIKE A SPILLED BOX OF FROOT LOOPS IN AISLE FOUR...

...BUT HERE WE ARE! INCREDIBLE, ISN'T IT??

INCREDIBLE.

MY ONE REAL MOMENT OF POWER IN THE RELATIONSHIP HAS COME AND GONE, AND I SPENT IT THINKING ABOUT HOW BAD MY HAIR LOOKED.

...SO YOU'RE A DOCTOR, NATHAN?

USED TO BE. I GAVE UP A HUGE PRACTICE SO I COULD ENJOY A SIMPLE, STRESSLESS LIFE.

YOU GAVE IT UP?

GAVE IT ALL UP! DUMPED THE HUGE HOUSE! DUMPED THE FANCY CAR! QUIT JETTING ALL OVER THE WORLD FIRST CLASS!

YEARS OF KILLING MYSELF TO IMPRESS WOMEN, SEDUCE WOMEN AND WIN WOMEN... AND WHAT DID IT GET ME?? HA, HA!!

WOMEN.

WELL, THERE **WAS** THAT...

PARDON ME. I HAVE A CHUNK OF HYPOCRISY STUCK IN MY THROAT.

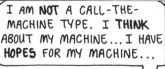

Panel 1:
WHY DON'T YOU JUST CALL YOUR MACHINE AND SEE IF HE LEFT A MESSAGE?

THERE ARE TWO KINDS OF PEOPLE, CHARLENE. THOSE WHO CALL THEIR MACHINES, AND THOSE WHO DON'T.

Panel 2:
I AM **NOT** A CALL-THE-MACHINE TYPE. I **THINK** ABOUT MY MACHINE... I HAVE **HOPES** FOR MY MACHINE...

Panel 3:
...BUT **CALL** MY MACHINE?? NEVER! IF MY MACHINE HAS SOMETHING TO SAY TO ME, I WANT TO BE STANDING RIGHT THERE TO LOVINGLY HEAR IT!!

Panel 4:
...AND IF NOT, SHE WANTS TO BE CLOSE BY SO SHE CAN **HIT** THE MACHINE.

JUST CALL ME A WOMAN WHO CRAVES PERSONAL CONTACT.

Panel 5:
I USED TO SPEND HOURS PREPARING FOR A MAN TO SEE MY HOME FOR THE FIRST TIME... BUT THAT WAS THEN, AND THIS IS...

Panel 6:
...OH, NO. I FORGOT HOW CUTE HE IS! I SHOULD HAVE SWEPT! I FORGOT HOW MUCH I LIKE HIM! I SHOULD HAVE DUSTED! I SHOULD HAVE FLUFFED!

Panel 7:
AACK!! TOO LATE!! HE'S HEADING FOR THE DOOR! HIDE THE DISHES! HIDE THE TRASH!! AACK!! HE'S ALMOST HERE HE'S...

Panel 8:
DING DONG

I EITHER NEED A LONGER MEMORY OR A LONGER SIDEWALK.

Panel 9:
SO HERE WE ARE, CATHY. A THIRD DATE!

THIS IS A THIRD **ENCOUNTER**, NATHAN. IT'S ONLY A **SECOND** DATE.

Panel 10:
BUT WE CAN **CALL** IT A THIRD DATE. WE CAN SKIP RIGHT OVER SECOND DATE WEIRDNESS AND CALL **THIS** A THIRD DATE!

YOU CAN'T SKIP A STEP! THIRD DATE ANXIETY CAN ONLY BE PROPERLY EXPERIENCED BY SURVIVORS OF SECOND DATE WEIRDNESS!

Panel 11:
SECOND DATE WEIRDNESS IS A CRITICAL TEST! YOU CAN BE WHERE YOU WISH, BUT NOW - AND FOR THE DURATION OF THE EVENING - **I** AM ON A SECOND DATE!!

Panel 12:
CURSES ON THE DAY I DREAMED OF MEETING A TRADITIONALIST.

Panel 1: IF YOU GAVE UP YOUR MEDICAL PRACTICE, WHAT DO YOU DO ALL DAY, NATHAN?

I DO WHAT PEOPLE WERE PUT ON EARTH TO DO, CATHY.

Panel 2: I TALK TO FRIENDS, READ, PLAY, LAUGH, STUDY, VISIT MUSEUMS, CREATE, LEARN, EXPLORE THE WORLD...

Panel 3: ...AND EVERY NOW AND THEN I EVEN STEP AWAY FROM MY COMPUTER FOR A BREATH OF FRESH AIR!

Panel 4: OH, HA, HA! BUT SERIOUSLY, WHAT DO YOU DO??

HOW QUICKLY WE GO FROM "GETTING TO KNOW YOU" TO "GETTING TO CREATE A WHOLE NEW VERSION OF YOU".

Panel 5: NATHAN WALKED PAST MY PHONE WITHOUT CHECKING HIS MESSAGES...HE'S PASSING MY TV WITHOUT CHECKING THE NEWS...PASSING MY SOUND SYSTEM WITHOUT CHECKING ANY GAME SCORES...

Panel 6: A MAN MADE IT THROUGH THE ELECTRONIC MAZE WITHOUT CHECKING ANYTHING! IT'S FINALLY HAPPENED! IT'S MY TURN! MY TIME! A WHOLE NEW ERA! IT'S...

Panel 7: beep beep beep- beep beep beep beep

Panel 8: ...WOMAN VS. THE WORLD WIDE WEB.

COOL! JUST LET ME CHECK MY MESSAGES, THE NEWS AND SOME SCORES!

Panel 9: I INVITED NATHAN IN AFTER DINNER AND HE MARCHED OVER TO MY COMPUTER AND SPENT TWO HOURS ON THE INTERNET!

MAYBE HE FELT SHY AND INSECURE.

Panel 10: MAYBE HE WAS INTIMIDATED BY YOU.

MAYBE HE WAS OVERWHELMED BY HIS ATTRACTION TO YOU AND JUST PANICKED.

Panel 11: YOU HAVE TO TRY AGAIN, CATHY! GIVE HIM A CHANCE! DON'T ABANDON THIS SENSITIVE, CARING SOUL OVER ONE LITTLE CASE OF SECOND DATE NERVES!!

Panel 12: ONCE A COFFEE ROOM. NOW A RELATIONSHIP RESUSCITATION ROOM.

1984: BRIAN CAME TO MY HOME. SPENT THE EVENING STARING LONGINGLY AT THE REFRIGERATOR.

1989: IRVING CAME TO MY HOME. SPENT THE EVENING STARING BLISSFULLY AT THE TV SET.

1996: NATHAN CAME TO MY HOME. SPENT THE EVENING STARING LUSTFULLY AT THE COMPUTER SCREEN.

A LIFETIME OF TRYING FOR A PERFECT WOMANLY SHAPE, AND I SHOULD HAVE JUST BEEN TRYING FOR A RECTANGLE.

HI, CATHY. IT'S NATHAN. I'M SO SORRY I SPENT THE EVENING ON THE INTERNET WHEN I WAS AT YOUR HOUSE.

IT'S OK. I UNDERSTAND.

IT'S INEXCUSABLE! THERE'S SO MUCH I WANT TO SHARE WITH YOU, AND I JUST SAT THERE WAITING FOR WEBSITES TO DOWNLOAD!

IT'S OK.

PLEASE LET ME MAKE IT UP TO YOU! PLEASE COME TO MY HOME AND GET TO KNOW THE REAL ME!

I'D LIKE THAT.

I HAVE AN ISDN LINE THAT'S FIVE TIMES FASTER THAN YOUR 28.8 MODEM AND A WAY HOTTER BROWSER! YOU WON'T BELIEVE HOW FAST I CAN RIP THROUGH CYBERSPACE!!

ANOTHER PERFECT FIRST THREE-FOURTHS OF A CONVERSATION...

WHERE'S ALL YOUR STUFF, NATHAN?

I'M STUFF-FREE, CATHY! YOU'RE STILL TRAPPED IN THAT WHOLE MATERIALISTIC RAT RACE THING, BUT I'M FREE!

I GOT RID OF CHAIRS I DIDN'T SIT ON... TABLES I DIDN'T USE... LAMPS I DIDN'T NEED... BOOKS I DIDN'T READ ... CLOTHES I DIDN'T WEAR... TVS I DIDN'T WATCH... AND ALL THE JUNK AND CLUTTER THAT DRIVES PEOPLE INSANE!

I RE-PRIORITIZED AND SIMPLIFIED UNTIL I GOT MY LIFE DOWN TO JUST ME AND MY LOVED ONES!

LOVED ONES?

...WELL, LOVED **ONE**, REALLY, BUT IT HAS A WHOLE BUNCH OF PEOPLE INSIDE.

LOOK AT THIS BEAUTY! PENTIUM-200 PROCESSOR WITH A 2 GIG HARD DISK... 32 MB OF EDO RAM AND 256 K OF CACHE... 128 BIT GRAPHICS ACCELERATOR CARD ... ISDN MODEM... AND RE-CORDABLE CD-ROM DRIVE!

LOOK AT THIS BEAUTY! SLEEK, NARROW-LEG PANTS ... SLINKY, BELTED, OPEN-NECK JERSEY TOP... SEN-SUOUS SUEDE FLATS... CAS-CADING HAIR... SULTRY CHARCOAL EYELIDS WITH GLIMMERY BRONZE LASHES!

SHOULD HAVE GOTTEN THE QUICK-TIME VR PLUG-IN.

SHOULD HAVE GOTTEN THE PLUM LIP LINER.

LOOK, CATHY!...click!... WE CAN READ MENUS FROM RESTAURANTS ALL OVER TOWN... ...click!... MODEM OUR ORDER TO BE DELIVERED...

UM, NATHAN?

...click!... PULL UP MOVIE CLIPS WHILE WE WAIT FOR OUR FOOD...click!...DROP A NOTE TO THE WHITE HOUSE ...click!... READ UP ON GARDEN FUNGUS...click!... ...PLAY CHESS...click!...

NATHAN... NATHAN!!

VISIT PLUTO!...click!... VISIT THE CIA!...click!... VISIT SEA WORLD!...click!...

NATHAN, COME UP FOR AIR! TAKE A BREAK! YOU HAVE COMPANY! YOU'RE ON A DATE!!

...click!...SHOP FOR SOFTWARE!...click!...COMPLAIN ABOUT WOMEN!...click!...

THE INTERNET: ALL THE THRILL OF PRO FOOTBALL, WITH NONE OF THE STATION BREAKS.

IT TURNS OUT NATHAN GAVE UP HIS MEDICAL PRACTICE TO SPEND TIME ON THE INTERNET, AND SOLD ALL HIS POSSESSIONS TO PAY HIS ONLINE BILLS!

A DOCTOR? YOUR BOYFRIEND IS A DOCTOR, CATHY??

HE'S AN EX-DOCTOR, MOM, AND HE ISN'T MY BOYFRIEND!

YOUR EX-BOYFRIEND IS AN EX-DOCTOR?

HE WAS NEVER MY BOYFRIEND! HE'S JUST A PERSON I USED TO THINK MIGHT HAVE POTENTIAL!

YOUR EX-POTENTIAL, EX-POSSIBLE-BOYFRIEND-PERSON IS AN EX-DOCTOR?

BINGO.

ANOTHER BLEAK YEAR FOR THE CHRISTMAS CARD LETTER.

DID YOU HAVE YOUR BREAKUP SCENE WITH NATHAN YET, CATHY?

THERE WON'T BE A SCENE, CHARLENE. WE ONLY HAD THREE DATES!

YOU'VE KNOWN HIM FOR A MONTH. THERE'LL BE A SCENE.

NOT AFTER THREE DATES! YOU HAVE TO HAVE SIX DATES BEFORE IT WARRANTS A SCENE.

UNLESS YOU'VE PASSED THE ONE-MONTH MARK. EVERY DAY PAST ONE MONTH NECESSITATES MORE OF A SCENE! EACH SECOND THAT GOES BY WITHOUT BREAKING UP MEANS THERE'LL BE A BIGGER SCENE!!

NATHAN, IT'S CATHY! I MUST SEE YOU IMMEDIATELY!

AM I IRRESISTIBLE, OR WHAT?

69

Panel 1: I CAN'T BREAK UP WITH NATHAN AS HE WALKS IN THE DOOR BECAUSE HE'LL FEEL HE'S BEING AMBUSHED.

HI.

Panel 2: I CAN'T BREAK UP AFTER WE'VE EXCHANGED PLEASANTRIES BECAUSE HE'LL FEEL DECEIVED.... I CAN'T BREAK UP AFTER WE'VE HAD A NICE DINNER BECAUSE HE'LL FEEL HUMILIATED....

Panel 3: ALL I CAN DO IS SPEND THE EVENING IN PRIVATE DISGUST, DREAMING OF SOME FUTURE TIME WHEN THE PERFECT OPENING IN WHICH TO DUMP HIM WILL PRESENT ITSELF.

Panel 4: HOW I HATE MY GENTLE, SENSITIVE SOUL.

LOOK, HONEY! I GOT OUR INITIALS PRINTED ON A MOUSE PAD!

Panel 5: I DON'T WANT TO GO OUT WITH YOU ANYMORE, NATHAN.

Panel 6: I HAVE NO INTEREST IN A MAN WHO'S GIVEN UP HIS WHOLE LIFE FOR THE INTERNET... NOR DO I CARE TO HELP YOU TRY TO DREDGE UP THE JEWEL OF A HUMAN THAT MAY STILL BE BURIED IN YOUR BRAIN UNDER 40,000 E-MAIL ADDRESSES!

Panel 7: THIS IS GOODBYE NATHAN! FAREWELL! FINITO! OVER! OVER AND OUT!

Panel 8: ...OH, IT FELT SO FABULOUS TO OPEN UP LIKE THAT! THANK YOU! I FEEL INCREDIBLE! THANK YOU!

WHAT DO YOU WANT TO DO TOMORROW NIGHT?

Bottom row:

MET IRVING. BOUGHT TWO DRESSES, FOUR JACKETS AND THREE PAIRS OF SHOES.

BROKE UP WITH IRVING. GOT RID OF FOUR SKIRTS, TWO BLOUSES AND A PURSE.

MET ALEX. BOUGHT SIX SWEAT-SUITS AND AN EVE-NING GOWN.

BROKE UP WITH ALEX. GOT RID OF THREE PAIRS OF PANTS AND A HAT.

MET NATHAN. BOUGHT TWO BLAZERS, A SKIRT AND TWO PAIRS OF BOOTS.

BROKE UP WITH NA-THAN. GOT RID OF SIX DRESSES.

SOME WOMEN HEAR VIOLINS. I SEE BAGS OF CLOTHES MOVING IN AND OUT OF THE HOUSE.

PLEASE QUIT WEEPING, MOM. IT'S OVER.

YOU WOULD HAVE MADE SUCH A BEAUTIFUL COUPLE!

I QUIT WEEPING. YOU CAN QUIT WEEPING.

HE NEVER GAVE YOU A CHANCE!!

HOW HAPPY COULD HE POSSIBLY BE WITHOUT ME?? THERE'S STILL HOPE! YOU TAUGHT ME THAT! THERE'S ALWAYS HOPE IF YOU LOOK IN THE RIGHT PLACE!!

DRESS HER FOR JOHN-JOHN ON THE REBOUND!!

GET IN LINE WITH ALL THE OTHER MOTHERS.

Fashion

NOTHING DEFINES FALL FASHION LIKE HEAD-TO-TOE SKINNY KNIT SWEATER DRESSING!

SKINN KNITS

SKINNY KNITTED PANTS... SLIM KNITTED SWEATERS... SLINKY KNITTED COATS... SVELTE KNITTED SKIRTS...

THEY'RE STRETCHABLE! VERSATILE! AND, BEST OF ALL, **PACKABLE!**

PACKABLE AND MOVE-OUT-OF-THE-COUNTRY-ABLE.

PRECISELY. AND IF YOU FIND SOMEPLACE WHERE BAGGY IS STILL IN, CALL COLLECT!

WHAT'S SO ALLURING ABOUT PLAIN BLACK JACKETS?

THOSE AREN'T BLACK. THEY'RE ALMOST-BLACK EGGPLANT... ALMOST-BLACK UMBER... ALMOST-BLACK NAVY BLUE...

THESE AREN'T BLACK?

SEE? SEE HOW YOU'RE DRAWN CLOSER TO TRY TO SEE THE REAL COLOR? SEE HOW YOU CAN'T GET QUITE CLOSE ENOUGH TO TELL THE DIFFERENCE?

SEE HOW A MAN WILL BE COMPELLED TO HURL HIMSELF ACROSS THE ROOM AND SMASH HIS EYES INTO YOUR SHOULDER TO FIGURE OUT WHAT COLOR YOU'RE WEARING?

IS THIS THE UMBER ONE OR THE BLUE ONE?

AT LAST! OUR MYSTIQUE IS BACK!

THIS YEAR SIMPLY UPDATE WHAT YOU OWN WITH A FEW BASIC PIECES!

SEE?? UPDATE YOUR SKIRT WITH THE NEW LONGER BLAZER... UPDATE YOUR BLOUSE WITH THE NEW BOOT-CUT PANTS...

UPDATE THE PANTS WITH THE NEW FITTED TURTLE-NECK... AND UPDATE THE WHOLE SHOW WITH THE NEW STACKED-HEEL BOOT!

YOU UPDATED ME RIGHT DOWN TO MY UNDER-WEAR.

ALSO HAS TO GO. VISIBLE PANTYLINE AND NOT NEAR-LY ENOUGH CHEST.

"KNIT TOP, $840"! HA, HA! THAT'S A GOOD ONE, CATHY!

"SKIRT $560"!! ARE THEY KIDDING, MOM?! HA, HA!!

"JACKET, $1495"!! HOO, HA! LOOK AT THAT ONE! HA, HA!!

"PANTS, $795"! "SHOES, $425"! WHAT A RIOT! HA, HA!

"MAGAZINE, $3.50"?? YOU PAID $3.50 FOR A MAGAZINE?!

FUNNY HOW UNFUNNY IT IS WHEN THE HUMOR GETS PERSONAL.

I BOUGHT THIS PRIM, ELEGANT SUIT LAST YEAR BECAUSE YOU CONVINCED ME IT WAS A CLASSIC!

IT IS A CLASSIC!

YOU'VE OWNED IT FOR A YEAR AND IT STILL HAS THE PRICE TAG ON IT... CLASSIC! YOU FANTASIZED YOU'D BE ABLE TO SQUISH INTO A SIZE 7 LAST WINTER... ...CLASSIC!

YOU DREAMED OF WEARING IT TO FICTITIOUS DINNER PARTIES THROWN BY YOUR HYPOTHETICAL FUTURE HUSBAND... CLASSIC!

AND NOW YOU HAVE A YEAR-OLD SUIT WITH AN EXPIRED TEN-DAY RETURN POLICY WHICH, OF COURSE, MAKES IT A...

CLASSIC.

WOMEN ARE SICK OF BUYING CLOTHES THAT ARE OUTDATED IN THREE MONTHS!

MILITANCE! PERFECT! SLIDE INTO THIS FALL'S NEW ARMY JACKET!

WE HAVE BETTER THINGS TO DO THAN WANDER AROUND THE MALL!

INDEPENDENCE! EXCELLENT! NOTHING SAYS IT BETTER THAN THE NEW NO-NONSENSE FLAT-FRONT PANT!

WE REFUSE TO BE FASHION VICTIMS ANYMORE!

INDIGNANCE! BRAVO! STOMP, STOMP, STOMP IN YOUR NEW WAFFLE-SOLED SUEDE JODHPUR BOOTS!

..RATS. I LOOK FABULOUS.

CONFIDENCE! YES! NOTHING HOLDS THE RECEIPTS AS WELL AS THE NEW UP-SIZED TOTE!

IT'S THE YEAR OF MULTIPLE-MAXI-DRESSING! A MAXI SKIRT UNDER A MAXI SWEATER UNDER A MAXI VEST UNDER A MAXI COAT!

OOPS.

ADD A CHUNKY BOOT ON A CHUNKY STEPLADDER ON TOP OF A PILE OF CHUNKY PHONE BOOKS ... AND TA, DA!

LOVELY AS LONG AS I STAND IN ONE SPOT.

WHEN YOU LOOK THIS GOOD, THE WORLD WILL COME TO YOU.

PATTERNED TIGHTS WILL MAKE THAT OUTFIT LOOK BRAND-NEW!

THE NEW LEG

HOW MUCH NEWER COULD IT LOOK? I JUST TRIED IT ON TWO SECONDS AGO!

AH, BUT YOU'RE WEARING IT WITH LAST YEAR'S LEG.

THIS ISN'T LAST YEAR'S LEG! THIS IS THE LEG I WAS BORN WITH!

PRECISELY. THE LEG IS ANCIENT. YOU CAN'T WEAR AN ANCIENT, FLESH-TONED LEG WITH A BRAND-NEW OUTFIT!

TO TRULY UNDERSTAND WOMEN'S FASHION, ONE MUST WITNESS THE MOMENT OF THE SALE...

Panel 1: I'VE BEEN TOO UPTIGHT, CHARLENE. I KNOW THAT. TOO PICKY. TOO GUARDED. TOO EMOTIONALLY ALOOF.

Panel 2: ...AND THEN IT HAPPENED. I HELD THE OATMEAL SUEDE ANKLE BOOTS IN MY ARMS AND I SAID YES.

Panel 3: I SAID **YES** TO THE STACKED-HEEL WING TIPS... **YES** TO THE PEARLIZED LEATHER RIDING BOOTS... **YES** TO THE BURGUNDY SQUARE-TOE CHUNKY PUMPS!! YES! YES! YES!

Panel 4: YOU'RE SUPPOSED TO SURRENDER TO LOVE, NOT THE SHOE DEPARTMENT.

I SURRENDERED TO SOMETHING. I SHOULD GET PARTIAL CREDIT.

Panel 5: THE PERSON TRACKING YOUR LOST PACKAGE IS ON ONE... THE TICKED-OFF CLIENT IS ON TWO... AND PEOPLE SELLING MOTIVATIONAL SEMINARS ARE ON THREE AND FOUR!

Panel 6: PAYROLL NEEDS A BETTER COPY OF THE $4.25 RECEIPT ON YOUR EXPENSE REPORT... PERSONNEL NEEDS A JOB SUMMARY AND BLACK-AND-WHITE PHOTO... AND I NEED $6.13 FOR YOUR PORTION OF FRAN'S BIRTHDAY CAKE!

Panel 7: HERE'S YOUR NEW VOICE MAIL GUIDE...NEW SOFTWARE UPGRADE... AND NEW INSURANCE MANUAL, FROM WHICH YOU NEED TO CHOOSE --AND COMPLETE THE TEN-PAGE QUESTIONNAIRE FOR-- YOUR PREFERRED HEALTH-CARE PROVIDER BY 2:00 PM!

Panel 8: IF I DIDN'T HAVE AN ACTUAL JOB TO DO, THERE'D ALMOST BE ENOUGH TIME TO WORK HERE.

Panel 9: I SHOULD ANSWER THESE CALLS WHILE I EAT LUNCH, BUT I CAN'T CALL WHILE MY MOUTH IS FULL...

Panel 10: I SHOULD WRITE THESE REPORTS WHILE I EAT, BUT I DON'T WANT TO DRIP SALAD DRESSING IN THE KEYBOARD...

Panel 11: I SHOULD BE FILING, ORGANIZING, OPENING MAIL... BUT I NEED TWO HANDS! EVERYTHING NEEDS TWO HANDS!!

Panel 12: ...SHOULD HAVE JUST GONE OUT TO LUNCH WITH ME.

WOULDN'T HAVE GOTTEN ANYTHING DONE.

Panel 1: LET'S BE TRANSITIONAL PEOPLE: SOMEONE TO DATE UNTIL THE REAL PERSON COMES ALONG.

BAD IDEA, NATHAN. LET'S JUST BE UN-ROMANTIC FRIENDS.

Panel 2: NO GOOD. LET'S BE SPECIAL EVENT ESCORTS.

NO WAY. LET'S BE LUNCH COMPANIONS.

NO INTEREST. LET'S BE E-MAIL PALS.

BLEAH. LET'S BE WORKOUT BUDDIES.

BLEAH.

Panel 3: THIS IS NEVER GOING TO HAPPEN IF YOU KEEP REPLACING MY IDEAS WITH YOUR LAME SUGGESTIONS! IF YOU'RE NOT WILLING TO MAKE AN EFFORT, JUST FORGET THE WHOLE THING!!

Panel 4: PEOPLE WHO SAY IT'S HARD TO MAKE A RELATIONSHIP WORK SHOULD TRY MAKING A NON-RELATIONSHIP WORK.

RING!

Panel 5: WE'VE OFFENDED THE BOZWELL CLIENT!

I'LL PUT THEM ON THE CORPORATE HOLIDAY GIFT BASKET LIST, MR. PINKLEY.

Panel 6: WE BLEW IT IN THE FINDLAY MEETING!

WE'LL MAKE SURE THEIR HOLIDAY CARDS ARE ALL SIGNED PERSONALLY BY OUR STAFF.

Panel 7: WHAT WILL WE DO ABOUT THE NEBLER FIASCO?!

IT'S TOO LATE TO AVOID THE DISASTER, BUT TOO EARLY TO SEND CHRISTMAS CHEER, SO WE'LL JUST RELAX AND ENJOY OUR LAST GUILT-FREE WINDOW IN 1996!

Panel 8: I LOVE A WORKER WHO BRINGS THE PERSONAL TOUCH TO BUSINESS.

TECHNICALLY, WE'RE FIVE WEEKS AHEAD OF SCHEDULE.

Panel 9: I HEAR YOU'VE SEEN NATHAN SOME MORE, CATHY. WHEN DO I GET TO MEET HIM??

WE ALREADY BROKE UP, MOM.

Panel 10: I KNOW YOU BOUGHT A NEW OUTFIT LAST WEEK. WHEN DO I GET A PEEK?

I ALREADY RETURNED IT.

Panel 11: A LITTLE BIRD TOLD ME YOU TRIED A NEW HAIRDO THIS MORNING...

IT'S OVER, MOM. THE WHOLE PHASE CAME AND WENT BY 9:15 AM.

Panel 12: MOTHERHOOD: ALL KNOWING, ZERO SEEING.

MY WHOLE DAY GOT WASTED ON INTER-OFFICE DRIVEL, AND NOW MY NIGHT'S BEING RUINED TRYING TO DO ALL MY WORK. THEREFORE, I DESERVE SOME ICE CREAM.

I DON'T **NEED** ICE CREAM. I DON'T EVEN **WANT** ICE CREAM. I SIMPLY **DESERVE** ICE CREAM.

CONSIDERING HOW OFTEN I'VE EATEN ICE CREAM WHEN I **DIDN'T** DESERVE IT, IT WOULD BE **WRONG** TO NOT HAVE IT NOW, WHEN IT'S SO JUSTIFIED! I **FORCE** MYSELF TO EAT THIS ICE CREAM AS AN ACT OF DEFIANCE AGAINST THE MORONIC FORCES THAT TRASHED MY DAY!!

WHILE THE WORLD SLEEPS, THE POWER OF RATIONALIZATION IS JUST STARTING TO WAKE UP.

THE SKIRT THAT GOES WITH THIS JACKET IS AT THE CLEANERS...

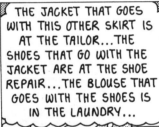

THE JACKET THAT GOES WITH THIS OTHER SKIRT IS AT THE TAILOR...THE SHOES THAT GO WITH THE JACKET ARE AT THE SHOE REPAIR...THE BLOUSE THAT GOES WITH THE SHOES IS IN THE LAUNDRY...

...AND THE PANTS THAT GO WITH EVERY SINGLE THING I OWN ARE IN DETENTION IN THE BOTTOM OF THE HAMPER FOR SHRINKING TWO SIZES.

CATHY'S READY TO COME TO THE OFFICE. HOWEVER, NONE OF HER CLOTHES HAVE SHOWN UP FOR WORK.

SEE THE SLEEK LINE THAT THE NEW LONG COAT FORMS OVER ALL YOUR LITTLE HUMAN RIPPLES AND INCONSISTENCIES?

SEE THE GRACEFUL MOVEMENT THE LONG COAT BRINGS TO EVEN THE LUMPIEST SWEATER DRESS?

SEE HOW YOU CAN TOSS A LONG COAT OVER THE DUMPIEST, FRUMPIEST OUTFIT AND SUDDENLY EXUDE ELEGANCE AND STYLE??

HI. MAY I HANG UP YOUR COAT?

NO.

QUICK, BOB! TELL ME HOW YOUR PERFORMANCE REVIEW WENT BEFORE I GO IN FOR MINE!

I ASKED FOR A 20% PAY CUT SO I CAN WORK 20% LESS, AND I GOT IT!!

YOU ASKED FOR LESS? YOU WERE SUPPOSED TO PAVE THE WAY FOR MORE!!

I GOT MORE! I GOT 20% MORE TIME FOR CHERYL AND ME TO PURSUE OUR LOVE OF COOKING!

TIME TO COOK?? YOU SET THE RAISE PRECEDENT AT TIME TO COOK??

NOTHING'S MORE REWARDING THAN CULTIVATING YOUR OWN GARDEN AND COOKING THE FRUITS OF YOUR HARVEST! GOOD LUCK!

GOODBYE, RAT RACE. HELLO, RATATOUILLE RACE.

TO NEGOTIATE YOUR RAISE:
1. RESEARCH YOUR COMPANY'S RAISE POLICY.
2. GET COMPARABLE STATISTICS FROM COMPETITORS.
3. PREPARE SUMMARY OF YOUR ACCOMPLISHMENTS.
4. DOCUMENT WAYS YOU'VE SAVED COMPANY MONEY.
5. ASSEMBLE PACKET OF COMMENDATIONS FROM CLIENTS.
6. ITEMIZE COURSES TAKEN AND NEW SKILLS ACQUIRED.
7. WRITE SYNOPSES OF SPECIAL PROJECTS.
8. PREPARE BULLET-POINT SHEET OF PERSONAL SACRIFICES.
9. PREPARE REBUTTAL FOR ALL CLICHÉD EXCUSES.

IF I HAD THE SORT OF JOB WHERE I HAD 100 FREE HOURS TO ASSEMBLE ALL THIS GARBAGE, I WOULDN'T BE SO DESERVING OF A RAISE!!

10. PRACTICE IN PRIVATE UNTIL YOU CAN DELIVER NUMBERS 1 THROUGH 9 WITH POISE AND DIGNITY.

BECAUSE OF THE FIVE WEEKENDS I SPENT REWRITING REPORTS AND EATING PIZZA IN MY OFFICE, WE DIDN'T LOSE THE McGUIRE BUSINESS!

BECAUSE OF THE FOUR SOLID WEEKS I STAYED HERE WITH A CALCULATOR AND A BOX OF FRIED CHICKEN UNTIL 9:00 P.M., WE SAVED THE NELSON ACCOUNT!

BECAUSE OF THE 200 FAST-FOOD LUNCHES I ATE AT MY DESK WHILE REWORKING PIE CHARTS, WE HUNG ON TO THE BIALKO DEAL!

I'VE EXCEEDED MY OWN PROJECTIONS BY FIVE POUNDS PER ACCOUNT.

NEVER LET IT BE SAID THIS COMPANY DOESN'T INSPIRE PERSONAL GROWTH.

"I'D LOVE TO GIVE YOU A RAISE, CATHY, BUT..."

"...THERE'S NO MONEY."

"PROFITS ARE IN THE TANK! TIMES ARE TOUGH! WE'RE ALL CUTTING BACK! MY HANDS ARE TIED!"

"IT KILLS ME TO KNOW THE PITTANCE YOU LIVE ON WHEN YOU'RE WORTH SO MUCH MORE, BUT WHAT CAN I DO?? THERE'S NO MONEY! NO MONEY AT ALL!"

MANAGEMENT MATERIAL!

"...WITH, UNFORTUNATELY, NO CHANGE IN INCOME, PERKS, OFFICE OR ACTUAL STATUS..."

LOOK AT ME, MR. PINKLEY. TWENTY NEW WRINKLES FROM THE FREID FIASCO.

NINETEEN NEW POUNDS FROM THE DRAKE DISASTER.

SIXTY-SEVEN MISCELLANEOUS BLOTCHES, BLEMISHES AND BULGES FROM SIXTY-SEVEN MISCELLANEOUS INTER-OFFICE BEEFS!

IF YOU CAN'T GIVE ME A RAISE, THEN GIVE ME LIPOSUCTION AND A FACE LIFT!!

RATS. SHE PRACTICED IN FRONT OF A MIRROR.

IN LIEU OF A RAISE, I'D LIKE TO ACQUAINT YOU WITH OUR NEW BENEFITS PACKAGE, CATHY.

BENEFITS PACKAGE?

FIRST, WE GIVE YOU "BENEFITS POINTS." THEN WE GIVE YOU BROCHURES ON THE HMO'S, PPO'S, POS'S, 401(K)s, LIFE INSURANCE PLANS, DISABILITY INSURANCE PLANS, DENTAL PLANS AND SALARY CONTINUATION PLANS.

IT WILL TAKE YOU MOST OF THE YEAR TO READ THE MATERIAL... AND BY THEN YOU'LL BE TOO DISGUSTED TO MAKE CHOICES SO YOU'LL SHOVE IT IN A DRAWER WHERE ALL THE OFFERS WILL EXPIRE!

ALL OF WHICH IS A GREAT BIG GIFT BACK TO THE COMPANY... THUS, THE "BENEFITS PACKAGE"!

NOTHING LIKE AN OFFICE THAT INSPIRES YOU TO GIVE 100%.

Panel 1: CONGRATULATIONS, CATHY! YOU CAN HAVE A TEENSY COST-OF-LIVING INCREASE WHOSE ONLY IMPACT ON YOUR SALARY WILL BE TO BUMP YOU INTO A HIGHER TAX BRACKET...

Panel 2: ...OR YOU CAN CHOOSE OUR BARE BONES BENEFITS PACKAGE, WHICH TAKES A CHUNK OF EVERY PAYCHECK AS YOUR MANDATORY EMPLOYEE CONTRIBUTION!

Panel 3: SEE?? YOU CAN HAVE LESS IMMEDIATELY, OR PLAN AHEAD TO HAVE LESS IN THE FUTURE! TWO UNBELIEVABLE CHOICES, AND EITHER ONE CAN BE ALL YOURS!!

THUNK

Panel 4: THE '90s BOSS: PART MANAGER, PART GAME SHOW HOST.

ANOTHER CONTESTANT JUST PASSED OUT FROM DELIRIUM, MR. PINKLEY.

Panel 5: "CHEAPNESS" IS AN UGLY WORD, CATHY, WITH ICKY CONNOTATIONS.

Panel 6: "FRUGALITY," ON THE OTHER HAND, IMPLIES A CERTAIN GENEROSITY OF INTENT EMBRACED BY BUDGETARY REALITIES AND SOUND BUSINESS PLANNING.

Panel 7: I KNOW THAT AS YOU PONDER YOUR LACK OF ANY ACTUAL RAISE, YOU'LL DO SO WITH GRATITUDE TOWARD A FRUGAL COMPANY WHICH USES ALL PROFITS TO INVEST IN A SAFE, SECURE FUTURE FOR US ALL!

Panel 8: FOR INSTANCE, THE LEASE ON YOUR NEW LEXUS.

DUAL AIR BAGS AND ANTI-THEFT PROTECTION. CAN'T BE TOO CAREFUL.

Panel 9: HOW'D IT GO, CATHY?

HOW DID WHAT GO, MOM?

Panel 10: IT. YOU KNOW...IT!

WHICH "IT"?

ANY OF THE "ITS"! I WANT TO KNOW HOW ALL THE "ITS" WENT!

Panel 11: MOM, I DIDN'T TELL YOU ANYTHING I WAS PLANNING TO DO THIS WEEK. YOU'RE JUST PRYING ON SPEC! IF I TOLD YOU ABOUT ANY OF THE "ITS" NOW, I'D ONLY BE REWARDING CONNIVING BEHAVIOR, AND I REFUSE TO DO THAT!!

Panel 12: HOW'D IT GO, DEAR?

FOILED BY MY OWN CREATION.

A DAY IN THE LIFE OF A DIETER

7:00AM – 9:00PM: VEGETARIAN

9:00PM – 12:00AM: CHOCOLATARIAN

chocolate

I CAN'T START MY CHRISTMAS CARDS THIS EARLY BECAUSE I'LL BE TEMPTED TO WRITE EVERYONE A LONG LETTER.

I THOUGHT YOU OWED EVERYONE A LONG LETTER.

I DO. BUT IF I ACTUALLY WRITE EVERYONE A LONG LETTER, THEY'LL JUST FEEL TERRIBLE BECAUSE THEY DON'T HAVE TIME TO WRITE LONG LETTERS BACK.

BETTER TO WAIT UNTIL THE LAST SECOND, GRAB SOME CARDS, SCRAWL MY NAME AND AN APOLOGY ON THEM AND LET MY LOVED ONES KNOW I'M JUST AS DISORGANIZED AND GUILT-RIDDEN AS THEY ARE !!

IT ISN'T EVEN THANKSGIVING YET, CATHY!

IT'S NEVER TOO EARLY FOR THE GIVING TO BEGIN, CHARLENE.

QUICK! SUSAN HAS THE "I CAN'T SHOW UP FOR THANKSGIVING WITH ORANGE HAIR" EMERGENCY!

FRAN HAS THE "I'VE GAINED 20 POUNDS SINCE THE LAST TIME I WAS HOME" EMERGENCY!

JIM HAS THE "I JUST BROKE UP WITH THE WOMAN MY PARENTS LOVE" EMERGENCY!

QUICK! BRAINSTORM! SUBMIT IDEAS! THURSDAY DEADLINE! EMERGENCY !!

CORPORATE AMERICA SCREECHES TO A HALT WHILE THE STAFF PREPARES TO EAT A MEAL WITH THEIR MOTHERS.

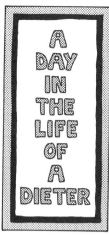

Panel 1:
WHAT CAN I BRING FOR THANKSGIVING, MOM?

OH, HEAVENS, SWEETIE! JUST BRING YOURSELF!

Panel 2:
...AND BRING ANY NEWS YOU MIGHT HAVE ABOUT DATING PROSPECTS... ...BRING PHOTOS OF ANY ROMANTIC INTERESTS...

Panel 3:
...AND BRING ANY THOUGHTS YOU HAVE ABOUT WHEN IT MIGHT ALL COME TOGETHER TO CREATE MARRIAGE AND GRANDCHILDREN!!

Panel 4:
WHILE THE WORLD BAKES PUMPKIN PIES, I WILL STAND IN MY KITCHEN AND ATTEMPT TO WHIP UP A LIFE.

Panel 5:
IF YOU'RE GOOD AT GRANDMA'S HOUSE, I'LL GIVE YOU THIS BISCUIT, ELECTRA.

Panel 6:
NO YAPPING, NO SLOBBERING, NO JUMPING, NO CHEWING... ...SHOW GRANDMA WHAT GOOD MANNERS YOU HAVE AND THIS GREAT BIG DOG BISCUIT IS ALL YOURS!!

Panel 7:
YAP SLOBBER JUMP CHEW YAP

GRANDMA'S LITTLE MONSTER IS HERE, AND I BAKED A NICE FRESH BATCH OF COOKIES FOR YOU!

Panel 8:
OUTBRIBED IN THE FIRST TWO SECONDS OF THE VISIT.

SORRY. NO SYMPATHY FROM ME. SHE BOUGHT MY SILENCE WITH A LOAF OF HOMEMADE NUTBREAD.

Panel 9:
YOU'RE THRILLED TO BE WITH DAD AND ME FOR THANKSGIVING, BUT PART OF YOU WONDERS IF YOU'LL EVER FEEL LIKE A GROWN-UP.

WHAT?? HOLD ON...

((chomp chomp))

Panel 10:
YOUR LIFE IS FULL AND REWARDING, BUT SITTING HERE AT THE ULTIMATE FAMILY MEAL, YOU SOMEHOW FEEL VAGUELY INCOMPLETE.

HOLD IT...WAIT...

((chomp chomp chomp))

Panel 11:
YOUR NEED TO REJECT ALL OUR OPINIONS ON THE SUBJECT IS MATCHED ONLY BY YOUR NEED TO HAVE OUR FULL APPROVAL.

WAIT!...WAIT!...

((chomp chomp)) chomp chomp))

Panel 12:
HOW MUCH MORE PIE MUST I EAT BEFORE MOTHER QUITS BEING ABLE TO SEE RIGHT THROUGH ME??

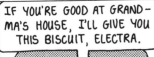

85

DO YOU HAVE A PEN SO I CAN CIRCLE...

OH, NO, NO..FIRST YOU NEED TO PUT STICKERS ON ALL THE GIFTS YOU THINK YOU'LL ORDER...

...THEN YOU PUT **DIFFERENT** COLORED STICKERS ON ALL THE HOLIDAY CRAFTS YOU FANTASIZE YOU'LL MAKE... ...THEN YOU PUT **DIFFERENT** COLORED STICKERS ON ALL THE HOLIDAY DISHES YOU PRETEND YOU'LL COOK...

...THEN YOU SPREAD THE STICKERED CATALOGS AND MAGAZINES ALL OVER THE HOUSE, WHERE THEY'LL STAY IN PRISTINE ARRANGEMENTS UNTIL NEXT FEBRUARY!

MY MOTHER: THE MARTHA STEWART OF "POST-IT NOTES."

AACK! SWEET POTATOES! I THOUGHT I GOT RID OF YOU ON MY POWER WALK YESTERDAY!

STUFFING!! WHO INVITED YOU??... DINNER ROLLS! WHAT ARE ALL YOU DINNER ROLLS STILL DOING HANGING AROUND MY WAIST??!

GET ME OUT OF HERE!! I'M SUFFOCATING! I CAN'T BREATHE! AAACK!!

COULDN'T TAKE THE HOLIDAY CROWD AT THE MALL?

COULDN'T TAKE THE CROWD IN THE HOLIDAY DRESS.

WHAT A NIGHTMARE! IT WAS CROWDED AND LOUD AND I DIDN'T KNOW WHAT WAS GOING ON FROM THE SECOND I GOT THERE!

WHEW! YOU TOO? I WAS HOT AND SWEATY AND DIZZY AND DISORIENTED...

...AND I WANTED TO RUN OUT SCREAMING BUT I COULDN'T **MOVE**! I WAS **TRAPPED**! I WAS **SQUASHED**! I NEEDED AIR I NEEDED SPACE I NEEDED WATER...

WHAT ARE YOU TWO TALKING ABOUT?

FOOTBALL STADIUM.

THE MALL.

MY WIFE WORKS FULL TIME, DRIVES THE KIDS ALL OVER THE PLACE AND HANDLES ALL THE MEALS AND HOUSE STUFF.... WHY SHOULD THE WHOLE BURDEN OF THE HOLIDAYS ALSO FALL ON HER??

SO I DID ALL OUR CHRISTMAS SHOPPING THIS YEAR! I MUST HAVE BEEN IN THAT MALL FOR 20 MINUTES, BUT I FOUND THREE OF THE THINGS ON THE LIST SHE MADE FOR ME!

I BROUGHT THEM HOME FOR HER TO WRAP, SO NOW ALL SHE HAS TO DEAL WITH ARE OUR CHRISTMAS CARDS, PARTY, AND WHATEVER SHE WANTS TO DO ABOUT THE THINGS I DIDN'T FIND!

WHEN THEY SPEAK OF A "'90s" MAN, THEY'RE REFERRING TO THE NUMBER OF SECONDS YOU CAN LISTEN TO ONE WITHOUT SCREAMING.

WHY NOT PRETEND IT'S CHRISTMAS EVE AND JUST START GRABBING GIFTS AT RANDOM, CATHY? YOUR SHOPPING COULD BE DONE IN AN HOUR!

IT WOULD SEEM SO INSINCERE, MOM.

BUT YOU'LL DO IT **ANYWAY**! YOU'LL WANDER AROUND FOR THREE WEEKS... CHRISTMAS EVE WILL COME... AND YOU'LL START GRABBING GIFTS AT RANDOM! IT WILL HAPPEN **ANYWAY**!

BUT WHEN IT HAPPENS ANYWAY, IT WILL BE THE **REAL THING**! IF I'M GOING TO INSULT MY LOVED ONES WITH LAST-MINUTE GIFT GRABBING, I INSIST UPON **AUTHENTIC** LAST-MINUTE GIFT GRABBING!!

OH, FOR CRYING OUT LOUD.

I AM NOTHING IF NOT GENUINE.

I MIGHT HAVE TO RESORT TO COMPUTER ADDRESS LABELS FOR MY CHRISTMAS CARDS THIS YEAR.

ARE YOU KIDDING?

CARDS

WE MOVED ON TO LASER PRINTED ENVELOPES LAST YEAR! YOU DON'T EVEN HAVE TO STICK ANYTHING ON!

WELL, YOU STILL HAVE ALL THE STAMPS.

STAMPS?? HOW ARCHAIC! THINK POSTAGE METER! PRINTED SIGNATURE! THE WHOLE SHOW CAN BE PRINTED AND MAILED WITHOUT YOU EVER TOUCHING A CARD! YOU'RE IN THE DARK AGES, CATHY!!

AS IF I WEREN'T BEHIND ON ENOUGH, NOW I'M BEHIND ON MY IMPERSONALIZATION.

CARDS

HOW COULD SHE INVITE ME TO LUNCH? WE HAD THE PERFECT FRIENDSHIP! WE NEVER GOT TOGETHER... HARDLY TALKED... WE JUST KNEW THE OTHER ONE WAS OUT THERE SOMEWHERE!

BUT WHAT COULD I SAY?? "NO, I DON'T THINK OF YOU AS A LUNCH FRIEND, JUST AN OCCASIONAL PHONE FRIEND"?? "NO, I LIKE YOU, BUT I DON'T WANT TO ACTUALLY HAVE TO SEE YOU"???

WHY DID SHE DO IT?? WE WERE SO HAPPY AS IT WAS! WHY DO PEOPLE ALWAYS TRY TO PUSH THE RELATIONSHIP TO THE NEXT LEVEL??

FOR ALL THEIR LOVE OF FOOTWEAR, WOMEN NEVER SEEM TO ENJOY IT WHEN THE SHOE IS ON THE OTHER FOOT.

NOTHING IS A MORE MEANINGFUL GIFT THAN THE MUSICAL TISSUE DISPENSER!

THE MUSICAL TISSUE DISPENSER?

BUY THIS AND YOU'LL HELP A RETAILER UNLOAD ITS STOCK... WHICH WILL HELP US STAY IN BUSINESS... CURB UNEMPLOYMENT... RAISE PUBLIC MORALE... AND BOLSTER SUPPORT OF STATE-FUNDED INSTITUTIONS!

WHAT COULD MEAN MORE TO THE RECIPIENT THAN KNOWING HIS OR HER CHILDREN WILL BE ASSURED A SOUND EDUCATION??

OK.

THE POLITICIANS HAVE HAD THEIR CHANCE. NOW IT'S UP TO THE SALESCLERKS.

MUSICAL TISSUE DISPENSERS

I WORK UNTIL 7:00PM. THE POST OFFICE CLOSES AT 5:00. WHEN AM I SUPPOSED TO BUY CHRISTMAS STAMPS??

I SPEND EVERY LUNCH HOUR ON HOLD WITH AN 800-OPERATOR. WHEN AM I SUPPOSED TO GET ALL THE OTHER HOLIDAY THINGS DONE THAT I'D NORMALLY DO DURING LUNCH??

I HAVE FOUR HOLIDAY EVENTS COMING UP, ALL SCHEDULED DURING PRIME SHOPPING HOURS. WHEN AM I SUPPOSED TO EVEN SHOP FOR THE OUTFITS TO WEAR TO THE EVENTS??

THE ANNUAL HOLIDAY CHALLENGE: TRYING TO SMASH A SIZE 16 SCHEDULE INTO A SIZE 2 TIME SLOT.

Row 1

NO TIME TO SHOP: GIFTS AREN'T BOUGHT.

CLOSED

NO TIME TO DECORATE: DECORATIONS AREN'T UP.

Christmas Decorations

NO TIME TO DO CARDS: CARDS AREN'T DONE.

CARDS CARDS CARDS CARDS CARDS CARDS CARDS CARDS

NO TIME TO EAT: HAVE SOMEHOW MANAGED TO GAIN SIX POUNDS.

THE HOLIDAY BODY: ONCE A REBEL, ALWAYS A REBEL.

Row 2

FOR MY DOG, MY LITTLE BABY, A SANTA CLAUS CHEW TOY!

RECEPTION

FOR MY DOG, MY SWEETHEART, A NEW FOOD AND WATER DISH!

FOR MY DOG, MY BEST FRIEND, A SET OF FOUR LITTLE RED BOOTS!

FOR MY DOG, MY THERAPIST, A TIN OF HOMEMADE BONE BISCUITS!

ANYTHING FOR THE PEOPLE IN YOUR LIFE?

MY DOG IS ALL THE PEOPLE IN MY LIFE.

RECEPTION

Row 3

I GOT YOU A LITTLE SOMETHING WHEN I WAS CHRISTMAS SHOPPING LAST NIGHT, CATHY.

A LITTLE SOMETHING?

RECEPTION

A LITTLE, CHEAP, JOKE SOMETHING... OR A LITTLE, EXPENSIVE SOMETHING...OR A LITTLE, INEXPENSIVE, YET MEANINGFUL SOMETHING??

RECEPTION

GIVE ME A HINT! GIVE ME SOME SHOPPING PARAMETERS!

OH, HA, HA! YOU'LL SEE! IT'S JUST PERFECT!

NOTHING RUINS THE HOLIDAYS LIKE A PENDING GIFT.

RECEPTION

QUICK! THE PARTY'S TO- NIGHT! I NEED A DRESS THAT TWIRLS AND SWIRLS! I NEED SHOES THAT PRANCE!

HURRY! I WANT TO **TWINKLE!** I WANT TO SHINE!!

AS I LAUGH AND CHAT AND DANCE I WANT TO SPARKLE FROM HEAD TO TOE! FASTER! FASTER!

HI!

DO YOU HAVE ANY PLACE WHERE I CAN GO LIE DOWN FOR A WHILE?

TOO MUCH STUFF! WHO'S GOING TO BUY ALL THIS STUFF?? WHO NEEDS ALL THIS STUFF??

THE STUFF ISN'T EVEN WHERE IT BELONGS! LOOK. THESE BEARS SHOULD BE OVER THERE! WALLETS GO THERE!

NOT ONE MORE THING MAY BE ORDERED BY THIS STORE UN- TIL EACH AND EVERY ITEM IS PUT AWAY PROPERLY OR TAKEN HOME BY SOME- ONE AND PUT TO GOOD USE!

MOM HAS LOST CONTROL OF HER OWN UNIVERSE, AND IS NOW TRYING TO REFORM THE MALL.

YOU'VE NEVER USED THIS VASE. WHY NOT GIVE IT TO BETH FOR CHRISTMAS, CATHY?

WHAT IF BETH'S SEEN IT IN MY CLOSET?

BETH'S NEVER BEEN TO YOUR HOME.

WHAT IF A MUTUAL FRIEND SEES THE VASE AND TELLS BETH SHE SAW IT IN MY CLOSET??

WHAT IF THE PERSON WHO GAVE ME THE VASE MEETS BETH SOME DAY, BECOMES A FRIEND, RECOGNIZES THE VASE AND TELLS BETH SHE GAVE IT TO ME! WHAT WOULD I SAY THEN, MOM?? WHAT WOULD I SAY??

CHRISTMAS '96 IS STILL UP IN THE AIR, BUT WE'RE AL- READY PLANNING FOR A PO- TENTIAL EVENT IN MAY, '98.

NOTHING TELLS YOUR LOVED ONES THEY'RE SPECIAL LIKE THE NEW UNISEX COLOGNES!

SEE? ONE SQUIRT, AND YOU'RE NOT A MAN, NOT A WOMAN, NOT A GIRL, NOT A BOY, NOT A GRANDMA, NOT A GRANDPA... JUST YOU!

YOU... A SPECIAL UNISEX HUMAN WHO SMELLS EXACTLY LIKE ALL THE OTHER SPECIAL UNISEX HUMANS!

IT'S THE FRAGRANCE OF THE '90s!

EAU DE IRONY.

AND FOR SPRING, EAU DE CLEARANCE SALE.

SORRY. WE'RE SOLD OUT OF ITEM 428Q.

YOU CAN'T BE SOLD OUT! I MARKED THIS PAGE ON NOVEMBER 27!

TODAY IS DECEMBER 19. WE'RE SOLD OUT.

BUT I KNEW I WANTED IT THREE WEEKS AGO! IT WAS THE ONE THING I WAS SURE I WANTED TO GET!

IT'S MINE, I TELL YOU! MINE!! IN MY HEART AND SOUL, I'VE ALREADY OWNED IT FOR WEEKS!!

IF ONLY GOOD INTENTIONS COULD BE GIFT WRAPPED.

CLOTHES TO IRON AND PACK. SHOES TO FIND AND PACK. GIFTS TO WRAP AND PACK.

CARD STUFF TO PACK. DOG STUFF TO PACK. WORK STUFF TO PACK. HAIR STUFF TO PACK.

WHY DON'T WE CELEBRATE CHRISTMAS AT MY HOUSE SOME YEAR, MOM?

DON'T BE SILLY, CATHY. WE'D HATE TO MAKE SUCH A BIG MESS IN YOUR HOME.

IF CATHY ROLLED HER CLOTHES INSTEAD OF FOLDING THEM, THEY WOULDN'T GET SO WRINKLED...BUT SHE DOESN'T WANT TO HEAR THAT FROM ME AGAIN.

IF SHE PACKED HER COSMETICS IN LITTLE PLASTIC BAGS, SHE WOULDN'T HAVE SUCH A MESS IF ONE SPILLED... ...BUT I WON'T SAY A WORD.

IF SHE KEPT LABELED ENVELOPES IN HER PURSE FOR ALL HER RECEIPTS SHE WOULDN'T HAVE SO MUCH TROUBLE FINDING EVERYTHING...BUT I WON'T UTTER A PEEP.

MUM'S THE WORD, BUT MOM'S THE ENCYCLOPEDIA.

TO LYNDA'S CAT FROM MY DOG...TO DIANE'S DOG FROM MY DOG...

TO CINDY'S BIRD FROM MY DOG...TO FRANK'S HAMSTER FROM MY DOG...TO ANDY'S DOG FROM MY DOG...TO SUE'S CAT FROM MY DOG...

I DID IT! I NOT ONLY CHECKED OFF THE HUMANS, BUT I COMPLETED THE PET GIFT EXCHANGE!!

LOUISE'S FISH HAD ELEVEN BABIES YESTERDAY! THEY EACH SENT OVER A LITTLE SOMETHING FOR YOUR DOG!

ARF ARF!

OH, NO, ELECTRA. THIS ISN'T FOR US. THIS IS CANDY WE PUT OUT IN CASE PEOPLE STOP BY.

PEOPLE DON'T EAT THE CANDY THEY PUT ON DISPLAY IN THEIR OWN HOMES...BUT IF THEY GO TO **OTHER** PEOPLE'S HOMES, THEY'RE **REQUIRED** TO EAT THE CANDY TO BE POLITE.

...AND, OF COURSE, IF PEOPLE COME HERE, WE **HAVE** TO EAT THE CANDY TO MAKE THE PEOPLE FEEL BETTER ABOUT THE FACT THAT **THEY'RE** EATING THE CANDY!

THE REST OF THE YEAR WE'RE ON OUR OWN, BUT DURING THE HOLIDAYS, FAT IS A GROUP EFFORT.

WE BOUGHT FEWER GIFTS, WROTE FEWER NOTES AND SENT FEWER CARDS...

WE SIMPLIFIED, SIMPLIFIED, SIMPLIFIED... AND NOW WE CAN SPEND A LOVELY, QUIET CHRISTMAS DAY DOING WHAT FAMILIES WERE MEANT TO DO...

WRITE BELATED CHRISTMAS CARDS AND THINK UP SOME FAST PRESENTS FOR ALL THE PEOPLE WE FEEL GUILTY ABOUT DUMPING FROM OUR LIST!!

AT LEAST THEY'RE STILL MOVING AS A UNIT.

WHEN THE GIFT ARRIVED, WE DIDN'T TOUCH IT.

WHEN SOMEONE ELSE ATE THE FIRST COOKIE, WE EACH TASTED ONE... WHEN IT GOT DOWN TO HALF FULL, WE SAMPLED ONE EVERY TIME WE WALKED BY....

NOW THAT IT'S DOWN TO THE LAST TWO LAYERS OF COOKIES, WE'RE DIVING IN WITH COMPLETE ABANDON.

THE LESS THERE IS, THE MORE WE EAT, MOTHER.

AMAZING HOW WE GAIN WEIGHT WHEN WE SUBSIST ON SO LITTLE.

GO RELAX, MOM. I'LL PUT THOSE IN THE DISHWASHER.

NO, THANKS. WHEN THERE ARE SO FEW, I JUST WASH THEM BY HAND.

YOU HAVE 75 CLEAN PLATES IN THE CUPBOARD. WHY NOT PUT THE DIRTY ONES IN THE DISHWASHER??

IT ONLY TAKES A FEW MINUTES TO DO THEM BY HAND.

IT TAKES **ZERO** MINUTES IF YOU PUT THEM IN THE DISHWASHER.

NONSENSE. YOU STILL HAVE TO SCRUB THEM WITH SOAP AND WATER FIRST.

AAGH!

WE WANT THE CHRISTMAS SPIRIT TO LAST ALL YEAR, BUT FIRST WE WANT IT TO LAST FOR TEN SOLID MINUTES IN THE KITCHEN.

JUST A SEC, DEAR. I'M TALKING TO CATHY ON THE PHONE.

ISN'T CATHY HERE IN OUR HOUSE?

YES! SHE'S TALKING TO ME ON THE PHONE IN THE BEDROOM!

WHY DON'T YOU JUST SIT IN THE SAME ROOM AND TALK?

WE WERE DRIVING EACH OTHER NUTS IN THE SAME ROOM, SO WE DECIDED TO TALK BY PHONE LIKE WE'RE MORE USED TO DOING.

WHAT?? THAT'S CRAZY! THAT'S THE CRAZIEST THING I EVER HEARD OF!!

OOPS. NOW I'VE DONE IT TO YOUR FATHER, CATHY.

JOIN THE PARTY AND PICK UP THE EXTENSION IN THE LIVING ROOM, DAD.

I GAINED NINE POUNDS AT YOUR HOUSE THIS YEAR, MOM!

NONSENSE. HOLIDAY AIR IS HEAVIER BECAUSE IT'S FILLED WITH PINE TREE AND CANDLE SCENTS, WHICH MAKE THE SCALE READ HIGHER.

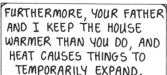

FURTHERMORE, YOUR FATHER AND I KEEP THE HOUSE WARMER THAN YOU DO, AND HEAT CAUSES THINGS TO TEMPORARILY EXPAND.

ALSO, THE EMOTIONS OF THE HOLIDAYS GET THE FAT CELLS ALL STIRRED UP AND DANCING AROUND, SO THEY APPEAR TO TAKE UP MORE SPACE. AS SOON AS YOU GO BACK TO YOUR REGULAR LIFE, THEY'LL ALL SETTLE BACK DOWN TO NORMAL!

OH.

THE '90s MOTHER: PART NURTURER, PART SCIENTIST.

I COULD DRESS IN SEQUINS AND DANCE NEW YEAR'S EVE AWAY AT A NIGHTCLUB...

I COULD SLITHER INTO AN EVENING GOWN AND DINE ON CHIC HORS D'OEUVRES AND CHAMPAGNE... GET DECKED OUT IN VELVET, OR...

...THEN AGAIN, I THINK I'LL JUST STAY HOME WITH YOU AND DAD.

THE WORLD OF GLAMOUR IS NO MATCH FOR A MOTHER WITH A PAN OF BROWNIES AND A SWEAT SUIT.

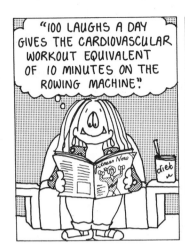

"100 LAUGHS A DAY GIVES THE CARDIOVASCULAR WORKOUT EQUIVALENT OF 10 MINUTES ON THE ROWING MACHINE."

HA!

ONLY 99 TO GO...

THE "GRAPE-FRUIT DIET": 3 WEEKS, AND IT WAS OVER.

THE "HEALTHY FOOD PLAN FOR LIFE": 60 MORE YEARS OF FAT-FREE SALAD DRESSING.

THE "HOLLY-WOOD DIET": 4 WEEKS, AND IT WAS OVER.

THE "HEALTHY FOOD PLAN FOR LIFE": 60 MORE YEARS OF BONELESS, SKIN-LESS CHICKEN BREAST.

THE "FRUIT JUICE FAST": 36 HOURS, AND IT WAS OVER.

THE "HEALTHY FOOD PLAN FOR LIFE": 60 MORE YEARS OF MELON BALLS FOR DESSERT.

CRASH DIETS NEVER WORKED, BUT AT LEAST THEY HAD AN END!

60 MORE YEARS OF BRAN FLAKES AND SKIM MILK!!

I CAN'T BELIEVE FAKE FAT TASTES SO GOOD!

THOSE AREN'T FAKE FAT, CATHY.

YOU SAID THEY WERE FAKE FAT.

NO. **THESE** ARE FAKE FAT! THE BAG YOU JUST ATE WAS REAL FAT!

I JUST ATE A BAG OF **REAL** FAT?? I THOUGHT I WAS EATING **FAKE** FAT!!

AACK! FALSE PRETENSE FAT! DO YOU HEAR THAT, BODY?? STOP THE PRESSES! IT'S **FALSE PRETENSE FAT!**

DON'T ASK.

WASN'T GOING TO.

MY BODY HAS FOUND ITS NATURAL WEIGHT, BUT I'M NOT HAPPY.

WHO IS THE "I" THAT ISN'T HAPPY? 99% OF ME IS MY BODY, AND MY **BODY'S** HAPPY. WHERE'S THE PART OF ME THAT **ISN'T** HAPPY??

WHICH MINUSCULE PART OF MY BRAIN IS CAUSING ALL THIS DISSATISFACTION?? WHICH ONE OF YOU IN THERE IS RESPONSIBLE FOR THIS MISERY?!!

I DON'T HAVE 17 EXTRA POUNDS. I HAVE ONE TOO MANY BRAIN CELLS.

I SAVED THESE PANTS TO REMIND MYSELF HOW FAT I USED TO BE, AND NOW I CAN'T GET THEM ZIPPED.

NOW I SAVE THEM TO REMIND MYSELF HOW THIN I USED TO BE.

THE PANTS THAT MARKED MY GRAND FAILURE ARE NOW THE SYMBOL OF MY FONDEST DREAM.

SOME PEOPLE HAVE WARDROBES. I HAVE A SCRAPBOOK ON HANGERS.

NO PIZZA. WE DON'T EAT PIZZA HERE!

WE ATE PIZZA LAST NIGHT.

NO ICE CREAM! ICE CREAM IS FORBIDDEN IN THIS HOME!

WE ATE ICE CREAM 18 HOURS AGO.

THIS IS A LOW-FAT, SUGAR-FREE, REDUCED-SODIUM, HIGH-FIBER HOUSEHOLD! VEGGIES FOR ME, DOG FOOD FOR YOU!

ELECTRA

I WAITED ALL DAY FOR MY PERSON TO COME HOME, AND NOW I HAVE TO WAIT FOR HER TO TURN BACK INTO HERSELF...

GET UP! EXERCISE! NOT FOR WEIGHT LOSS. EXERCISE FOR **HEALTH**!

...NO. NOT FOR HEALTH. EXERCISE FOR **RADIANT SKIN**! ...NO. NOT FOR SKIN. EXERCISE FOR THE **JOY OF MOVEMENT**!

...NO. NOT FOR MOVEMENT. EXERCISE FOR AN **IMPROVED LOVE LIFE**! YES! **LOVE**! DO IT FOR **LOVE**!!

DAY 1 OF THE FITNESS PROGRAM: 20 SECONDS ON MY TREADMILL, 20 MINUTES ON MY INCENTIVE.

NO VISIBLE PROGRESS. NO INCREASED STRENGTH.

NO CHEERING CROWD. NO PROUD COACH.

JUST ME, ALONE IN THE LIVING ROOM, WITH ONE SORE MUSCLE SOMEWHERE UNDER THE FAT AND SOME CHEERY PROMISES WRITTEN ON THE SIDE OF A CARDBOARD BOX.

SAY WHAT THEY WILL ABOUT OLYMPIC ATHLETES, THE REAL MEDALS SHOULD GO TO THOSE WHO GET OUT THE AB MACHINE ON DAY TWO.

NO! DON'T STOP AT ANOTHER TREE, ELECTRA! WE HAVE A 5K WALK TO DO!

NO! DON'T STICK YOUR NOSE IN THAT BUSH! WE HAVE TO MOVE! WE HAVE TO PUMP! QUIT SMELLING EVERYTHING!

COME ON! YOU CAN'T ACCELERATE YOUR HEART-RATE IF YOU STOP EVERY TWO FEET! COME ON! MOVE!

FITNESS REGIME OF THE DOG OWNER: POWER SNIFFING.

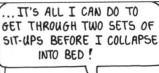

Panel 1: IT'S SO HARD TO MAKE MYSELF EXERCISE AFTER WORK, BUT I'VE BEEN DOING IT! / WHEW! ME TOO, CATHY.

Panel 2: I FACE TWO WILD PRESCHOOLERS AT THE DOOR... WE HAVE PLAY TIME, DINNER TIME, DISH-WASH TIME, BATH TIME AND STORY TIME... THEN I MAKE TOMORROW'S LUNCHES, PICK UP ALL THE TOYS, DO A LOAD OF WASH AND SPEND TIME WITH MY HUSBAND...

Panel 3: ...IT'S ALL I CAN DO TO GET THROUGH TWO SETS OF SIT-UPS BEFORE I COLLAPSE INTO BED!

Panel 4: I FACE A REALLY COMFY COUCH!!

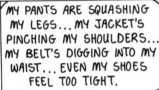

Panel 5: MY PANTS ARE SQUASHING MY LEGS... MY JACKET'S PINCHING MY SHOULDERS... MY BELT'S DIGGING INTO MY WAIST... EVEN MY SHOES FEEL TOO TIGHT.

Panel 6: IT HURTS TO WALK. IT'S AGONY TO SIT.

Panel 7: WHY DON'T YOU COME TO THE GYM WITH ME DURING LUNCH?

Panel 8: DON'T WANT TO EXPERIENCE ANY DISCOMFORT.

Panel 9: CHARLENE BEGGED ME TO TRY HER STEP CLASS, SO I SAID, "WHY NOT?" / ME, TOO. WHY NOT?

Panel 10: I SPENT LAST NIGHT WITH SUE'S TORTURE AB VIDEO. HOW MUCH WORSE CAN A STEP CLASS BE? / I'VE TRIED LYNN'S BUTT MACHINE AND KIM'S CLIMBING MACHINE. THERE HAS TO BE SOMETHING BETTER OUT THERE.

Panel 11: I'VE BEEN BORED, DISGUSTED AND HUMILIATED, BUT I WILL KEEP AN OPEN, LOVING MIND UNTIL I FIND SOMETHING I CAN STAND!

Panel 12: WE'VE GIVEN UP ON MEN, AND ARE GOING ON BLIND DATES WITH EXERCISE EQUIPMENT.

THERE'S PART OF A MUFFIN ON THE KITCHEN COUNTER, BUT WE WON'T THINK ABOUT IT, ELECTRA.

WE WON'T THINK ABOUT IT BECAUSE WE SATISFIED OUR MUFFIN URGE WITH HALF A MUFFIN EARLIER, AND WE'RE SAVING THE SECOND HALF FOR TOMORROW.

BY REAFFIRMING OUR LACK OF INTEREST IN THE MUFFIN, WE'RE FREE TO GO INTO THE KITCHEN FOR A GLASS OF WATER WITHOUT.....

TO DO TOMORROW: FIND A DIET BUDDY WHO CAN'T OUTRUN ME.

FIFTEEN YEARS OF ANALYZING THE PSYCHOLOGY OF OVEREATING... AND I'VE NEVER STAYED ON A DIET FOR A FULL MONTH.

FIFTEEN YEARS OF STAYING ON THE CUTTING EDGE OF RESEARCH ON METABOLISM AND FOOD ABSORPTION...AND I'VE NEVER YET LASTED ON A FITNESS PROGRAM FOR TWO WEEKS STRAIGHT.

FIFTEEN YEARS OF SEMINARS, WORKSHOPS AND CONSULTATIONS WITH EXPERTS...AND THE BEST I'VE EVER DONE IS TO BE FAIRLY GOOD BETWEEN 8:00 AND 11:00 AM.

I HAVE A GRADUATE DEGREE IN WEIGHT LOSS, BUT MY FAT IS STILL STUCK IN PRESCHOOL.

I KNOW APPROXIMATELY HOW MUCH I SPENT ON CHRISTMAS, SO OPENING THE BILLS WON'T BE A HUGE SHOCK.

TO LESSEN THE BLOW, I'LL DOUBLE THE AMOUNT I THINK IT IS... ...TO ENSURE THAT I'LL BE PLEASANTLY SURPRISED, I'LL TRIPLE IT.

I AM NOW VISUALIZING A NUMBER SO HIDEOUS THAT, BY COMPARISON, THE ACTUAL BILLS CAN ONLY BRING TOTAL RELIEF AND JOY.

RACK

OR NOT.

JANE: BEGAN THE DAY WITH A ONE-HOUR "STEP-N-TONE" CLASS.

TED: BEGAN THE DAY WITH A ONE-HOUR "CARDIO FUNK" CLASS.

CATHY: BEGAN THE DAY BY OPENING HER POST-HOLIDAY BILLS.

FACING THE MUSIC IS TEN TIMES MORE EXHAUSTING THAN EXERCISING TO IT.

QUICK! WATER! SHE NEEDS REHYDRATION!

YOU OVERSPENT ON THE HOLIDAYS AND THE BILLS ARE FLYING IN FROM EVERY DIRECTION.

THE HORROR OF EACH EXCESSIVE PURCHASE IS MULTIPLIED BY THE NAUSEA OF KNOWING EACH DEBT IS COMPOUNDING AT 18% INTEREST.

BUT HELP AWAITS! JUST PICK UP THE PHONE AND MAKE THE CALL THAT CAN START YOU ON A WHOLE NEW FINANCIAL TRACK!

HELLO, CHARLENE? HOW MUCH DID YOU LIKE YOUR CHRISTMAS PRESENT? ...ALSO, IS THE PRICE TAG STILL ATTACHED??

I HAVE TO FIND A FINANCIAL ADVISER, CHARLENE!

FOR WHAT?

FOR ME! I'M A HOPELESS MESS OF UNPAID BILLS... UNBALANCED CHECKBOOKS... UNMADE INVESTMENTS... I WANT TO START OVER! I WANT SOMEONE TO HELP ME GET BACK TO ZERO!

HOW MUCH MONEY DO YOU HAVE TO WORK WITH?

ZERO.

WISH GRANTED!

I WANT TO PAY SOMEONE TO TELL ME THAT!

I NEVER KNOW WHAT THE BALANCE IS IN MY CHECKBOOK, AND I AM SICK OF IT!

WITH MY NEW "CHECKBOOK MANAGER" SOFTWARE, I COMMIT TO A LIFE WHERE, EVERY MINUTE OF EVERY DAY, I KNOW TO THE PENNY HOW MUCH I HAVE IN THE BANK!

CLICK!

STEP ONE: ENTER YOUR CURRENT CHECKBOOK BALANCE.

I CAN'T DO STEP ONE, "ENTER CURRENT CHECKBOOK BALANCE", BECAUSE I DON'T **KNOW** MY CURRENT CHECKBOOK BALANCE!

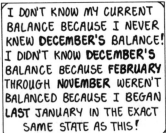

I DON'T KNOW MY CURRENT BALANCE BECAUSE I NEVER KNEW **DECEMBER'S** BALANCE! I DIDN'T KNOW **DECEMBER'S** BALANCE BECAUSE **FEBRUARY** THROUGH **NOVEMBER** WEREN'T BALANCED BECAUSE I BEGAN **LAST JANUARY** IN THE EXACT SAME STATE AS THIS!

IF I WERE THE SORT OF PERSON WHO KNEW MY BALANCE, I WOULDN'T BE THE SORT WHO'D WASTE $60 ON A USELESS PROGRAM LIKE YOU!!

IF SOFTWARE WERE REALLY USER FRIENDLY, STEP TWO WOULD INCLUDE A MASSAGE AND A NICE HOT CUP OF COCOA.

PARKING METER: 10¢.

CLINK!

ONE MOMENT, WHILE I STEP INSIDE THIS WARM BUILDING TO ENTER IT IN MY FINANCIAL JOURNAL.

FIRST I RECORD HOW MUCH I SPENT, WHY I SPENT IT AND MY FEELINGS ABOUT SPENDING IT... THEN I LOG THE EXPENSE ONTO MY IN-PURSE SPREADSHEET AND CALCULATE A NEW CASH BALANCE FOR MY WALLET....

LOBBY

...AT LAST! FINANCIAL CONTROL!!

PARKING TICKET: $25.

THIS HOMEMADE SANDWICH COST ABOUT 50¢. A CARRY-OUT SANDWICH COSTS $5.00.

WHY NOT JUST BRING OUR LUNCHES **EVERY** DAY?? WHY PAY $4.50 MORE FOR THE SAME SANDWICH??

BECAUSE WHEN WE BRING OUR LUNCHES, WE EAT THEM BY 9:30AM.

THE $4.50 EXTRA THE RESTAURANT CHARGES IS TO GUARD THE FOOD UNTIL LUNCHTIME.

ALL I HAVE LEFT TO SUSTAIN ME UNTIL DINNER IS A CARROT.

$100?? I'M NOT WASTING $100 ON A FINANCIAL CONSULTANT!

YOU'VE SPENT $100 ON WORSE THINGS, CATHY.

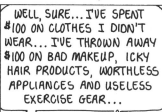

WELL, SURE... I'VE SPENT $100 ON CLOTHES I DIDN'T WEAR... I'VE THROWN AWAY $100 ON BAD MAKEUP, ICKY HAIR PRODUCTS, WORTHLESS APPLIANCES AND USELESS EXERCISE GEAR...

...BUT I DRAW THE LINE AT SPENDING $100 ON A HUMAN!

WE ALL HAVE OUR THRESH-HOLD.

IF I'M GOING TO BLOW $100, I WANT THERE TO BE SOMETHING TO SHOW FOR IT STUFFED IN A BOX IN MY BASEMENT.

I'VE BEEN GOOD ON MY DIET AND BUDGET ALL WEEK. I DESERVE TO BLOW $3.00 ON A DECADENT SNACK!

EXPRESS CHEC

...HURRY UP! MY RATIONALIZATION LEVEL IS HIGH! RING ME UP BEFORE I GET STRONG AGAIN!!

EXPRESS CHEC

...AACK! MY WILLPOWER IS TRYING TO DRAG ME AWAY AND MAKE ME TRADE MY ICE CREAM FOR AN APPLE! HURRY! I DON'T WANT TO BE GOOD! RING ME UP BEFORE...

....EXPRESS LANE, INDEED.

EXPRESS CHECK·O

I HATE THE STEREOTYPE OF WOMEN WHO CAN'T MANAGE THEIR MONEY!

ME TOO!

BUT I DON'T MANAGE MY MONEY.

ME EITHER.

I'M ASHAMED, BUT NOT ASHAMED ENOUGH TO ADD "LEARN ABOUT THE ASTOUNDINGLY BORING WORLD OF FINANCE" TO MY ALREADY BACKBREAKING LIST OF THINGS TO DO!!

I HATE THE STEREOTYPE OF WOMEN WHO JUSTIFY LAZINESS BY FINDING GIRLFRIENDS WHO AGREE WITH THEM.

ME TOO.

YOU'RE RIGHT, MOM. I OVERSPENT ON THE HOLIDAYS. THEREFORE, MY NEW SWEATER, NEW SHOES AND NEW JACKET GO BACK!

...WAY TO THE BACK OF THE SWEATER DRAWER... WAY TO THE BACK OF THE SHOE BOX PILE... AND WAY TO THE BACK OF THE CLOSET...

...THEN I'LL SNEAK THE PRICE TAGS OUTSIDE AND STUFF THEM WAY IN THE BACK OF THE TRASH CAN!

...DID EVERYTHING GO BACK, CATHY?

EVERYTHING WENT BACK.

SINGLE PEOPLE CAN'T MEET ANYONE UNTIL THEY'RE HAPPY ON THEIR OWN, CATHY.

NOT ANYMORE, MOM. NOW WE'RE ALL TOO HAPPY.

WE GO HOME...THROW ON OUR SWEATS...LIE ON OUR SOFAS WITH PLATES OF CARRY-OUT ON OUR STOMACHS...PUT ON OUR MOVIES AND TURN ON OUR ANSWERING MACHINES...

WHO WANTS TO GO OUT?? WHO NEEDS THE AGGRAVATION?? WE'RE ALL PERFECTLY HAPPY DRIFTING OFF IN OUR OWN LITTLE COCOONS!!

FORGET, MR. RIGHT. NOW WE'RE LOOKING FOR MR. AWAKE.

Row 1

 MY VALENTINE'S WEEK AFFIRMATIONS: I AM DESERVING OF LOVE! I AM OPEN TO LOVE! I ATTRACT LOVE BECAUSE I RADIATE LOVE!

 ... I'VE **ALWAYS** RADIATED LOVE! I SHOULD HAVE HAD LOVE LONG BEFORE THIS!

 I **COULD** HAVE HAD LOVE BEFORE, BUT THE OTHER PERSON BLEW IT! THIS TIME **I** CALL THE SHOTS! IT'S **MY** TURN! **MY** TURN FOR LOVE!!!

THERE'S A REASON THEY SUGGEST DOING AFFIRMATIONS IN THE PRIVACY OF YOUR OWN HOME....

WOULDN'T WANT ALL THESE GOOD VIBES TO GET TRAPPED INSIDE.

Row 2

 THE LAST TIME I HAD A REALLY GOOD VALENTINE'S DAY WAS IN KINDERGARTEN.

VALENTINE GIFTS

 BY AGE SIX, THE BOYS ALL GOT WEIRD.

WE ONLY GOT WEIRD BECAUSE ALL THE GIRLS GOT MUSHY.

WE GOT MUSHY BECAUSE YOU STARTED IGNORING US!

WE IGNORED YOU BECAUSE YOU LOST YOUR SENSES OF HUMOR!

WE LOST OUR SENSES OF HUMOR BECAUSE YOU PUT DEAD BUGS IN OUR VALENTINES!

 HA, HA! COOL! I FORGOT ABOUT THAT ONE!

FOR MEANINGFUL DIALOGUE, WE HAVE TO THINK BACK TO PRESCHOOL...

Row 3

 IF YOU THOUGHT YOUR HUSBAND WOULD LOVE A BOOK OF ROMANTIC POEMS FOR VALENTINE'S DAY AND HE DIDN'T, YOU WOULD...

BE ANNOYED! IT'S A BEAUTIFUL GIFT!

 IF YOUR HUSBAND THOUGHT YOU'D LOVE NEW SPEAKERS AND YOU DIDN'T, YOU WOULD...

BE HURT BECAUSE HE DOESN'T KNOW ME AT ALL!

 IN OTHER WORDS, IF THE **WOMAN** DOESN'T UNDERSTAND THE **MAN**, IT'S THE **MAN'S** FAULT... AND IF THE **MAN** DOESN'T UNDERSTAND THE **WOMAN**, IT'S THE **MAN'S** FAULT?!!

 WHAT'S HIS PROBLEM?

DON'T KNOW. MEN ALWAYS SEEM SO IRKED RIGHT AT THE MOMENT OF REALIZATION.

I'M READY TO MEET SOMEONE, CHARLENE. THERE. I SAID IT. I PUT IT OUT TO THE UNIVERSE.

YOU MUMBLED IT TO THE UNIVERSE, CATHY. DOESN'T COUNT.

IF YOU WANT THE UNIVERSE TO LISTEN, YOU HAVE TO SCREAM IT WITH ALL YOUR HEART!

I'M READY TO MEET SOME-ONE!!

EXCEPT YOU HAVE TO SIMUL-TANEOUSLY ACT DISINTEREST-ED SO THE UNIVERSE WON'T THINK YOU'RE DESPERATE.

IS THERE NOTHING LEFT IN LIFE THAT ISN'T A MULTI-TASK?

TO ME, BECAUSE I DESERVE IT!

TO IRVING, FOR NOT APPRECIATING ME.... TO ALEX, FOR NOT UNDERSTANDING ME...

AND TO THE TEN MILLION MEN OUT THERE WHO ARE WHINING ABOUT THE LACK OF GOOD WOMEN WHILE DOING ABSOLUTELY NOTH-ING TO MEET ME, THE PERFECT ONE!!

LIFE IS SO MUCH RICHER WHEN WE THINK OF OTHERS.

MONEY SAVED NOT BUYING VALENTINE GIFTS FOR A MAN, VALENTINE CARDS FOR A MAN OR VALENTINE OUT-FITS TO LOOK BEAUTIFUL FOR A MAN: $543.72.

MONEY SPENT CONSOLING SELF, VINDICATING SELF, HONORING SELF, REINVEST-ING IN SELF AND GENERALLY PUMPING SELF UP: $543.72.

MY CHECKBOOK MAY NEVER BALANCE, BUT MY LIFE ALWAYS COMES OUT TO THE PENNY.

LAPTOP COMPUTER, DENOTING ME AS A WORKING WOMAN ...TRAVEL BROCHURE, INDICATING MY LOVE OF TRAVEL, ...HEART-SHAPED NOTE PAD, SHOWING MY ROMANTIC SIDE...

I WILL NOW READ MY BOOK ON DOGS WHILE I RAISE MY ACTIVE-WEAR-CLAD ARM AND GESTURE WITH MY RINGLESS FINGER FOR THE WAITER TO BRING ME A HEALTH-CONSCIOUS, FAT-FREE SCONE!

THE COFFEE SHOP: ONCE, A PLACE TO DRINK COFFEE. NOW, A SINGLE PERSON'S PROMOTIONAL DISPLAY AREA.

HE'S CUTE. I COULD SAY HELLO.

...EXCEPT THERE'S A CELL PHONE STICKING OUT OF HIS POCKET. BAD SIGN.... AND WHY THE GEEKY SHIRT??

...AND WHAT HIDEOUS RELATIONSHIP HAS HE BEEN IN THAT'S MADE HIM NEED TO REBEL AND WEAR OLIVE DRESS SOCKS WITH CROSS-TRAINING SHOES... AND DO I WANT TO SPEND THE REST OF MY DAYS HELPING HIM BECOME HUMAN AGAIN?!

ANOTHER '90s WOMAN FACES A WINDOW OF OPPORTUNITY AND STOPS TO DISINFECT IT.

...ALSO, TOO INSENSITIVE! NO RESPONSE WHATSOEVER TO SUBTLE FLIRTATION!

I HATE DATING.

ME TOO.

HATE THE EXPECTATIONS. HATE THE MANDATORY PHONY CHEERFULNESS. HATE EVERYTHING ABOUT IT.

ME TOO.

THE ONE AND ONLY REASON I'LL GO ON A DATE IS TO GET IT OVER WITH SO I WON'T HAVE TO DO IT ANYMORE!

ME TOO.

LEAVE IT TO THE '90s TO TURN ROMANCE INTO A FORM OF EXERCISE.

THE OFFICE HAS OFFICIALLY DIVIDED INTO OUR WINTER FLU TEAMS, MR. PINKLEY.

THE "PARANOIDS" ALL WENT HOME AT THE FIRST TWINGE AND ARE LYING IN BED DEMANDING ANTIBIOTICS...

THE "HERBALISTS" ARE STANDING OUTSIDE IN TEN-DEGREE "FRESH AIR," STUFFING DOWN ECHINACEA...

THE "DENIALS" ARE STAGGERING AROUND CONTAMINATING EVERYTHING WHILE REFUSING TO TREAT THEIR SYMPTOMS...

MUST THIS OFFICE SCREECH TO A HALT OVER A FEW GERMS?

I'LL PUT YOU DOWN FOR THE "SELF-RIGHTEOUS" TEAM. YOU'LL BE RECEIVING YOUR FEVER IN A FEW HOURS.

ACHOO!

I FEEL TERRIBLE. HEADACHE... SORE THROAT... CHILLS...

AACK! GET AWAY FROM ME!!

DID YOU TOUCH THIS MEMO? DID YOU BREATHE ON MY PHONE MESSAGE??

WHERE'S THE DISINFECTANT?? WHERE'S THE ANTIBACTERIAL SCRUB?? HOLD YOUR BREATH UNTIL WE CAN STERILIZE THE AREA!!

WHY DIDN'T YOU STAY AT HOME TODAY, CHARLENE?

COULDN'T GET ANY SYMPATHY AT HOME.

LITTLE SAM, MY 14-MONTH-OLD, BROUGHT HOME A FLU BUG FROM PLAYGROUP, AND I WAS SICK FOR A WEEK!

OH, POOR THING! IS SAM FEELING BETTER?

LITTLE SARA, MY THREE-YEAR-OLD, BROUGHT HOME A BRONCHITIS BUG FROM PRESCHOOL, AND THE WHOLE FAMILY CAUGHT IT!

HOW AWFUL! DO YOU NEED ANY HELP?

LITTLE ELECTRA, MY DOG, BROUGHT HOME FLEAS FROM THE PARK, AND I'VE BEEN ITCHING FOR A MONTH!

BLEAH! THAT'S DISGUSTING!!

WHEN YOU'RE SINGLE, EVEN YOUR BUGS DON'T GET INCLUDED IN THE GROUP.

WHEW... THAT WAS THE WORST FLU I EVER HAD!

HAH! YOU ONLY HAD THE **LITTLE** FLU. I HAD THE REALLY **BAD ONE!**

ARE YOU KIDDING? I WAS IN BED FOR A WEEK!

I WAS IN BED FOR **TEN DAYS!**

I COULD BARELY LIFT MY ARM!

I COULDN'T MOVE AT ALL!

I HAD TO REST FOR AN HOUR AFTER A SIP OF WATER!

I COULDN'T HOLD A GLASS!

1997: THE MOST PHYSICALLY FIT GENERATION IN HISTORY TURNS COMPLETE IMMOBILITY INTO A COMPETITIVE SPORT.

I WAS TOO WEAK TO PUSH THE REMOTE!

I COULDN'T LIFT MY EYELID!

IS MY OLD DOCTOR ON OUR NEW HEALTH PLAN, AND IF SO, DO I PAY NOTHING, PAY PART, OR PAY THE DEDUCTIBLE... AND IS IT LIKE MY CAR, WHERE MY PREMIUM WILL GO UP IF I SAY "BOO"?

DO I ASK MY DOCTOR OR ASK THE INSURANCE COMPANY...OR DOES SOMEONE KNOW WHERE THAT LITTLE BOOKLET IS THAT LISTS THE "PREFERRED" DOCTORS?

IF MY DOCTOR'S NOT PREFERRED, HAS ANYONE IN OUR OFFICE EVER HEARD OF ANY OF THE DOCTORS WHO ARE?... KEEPING IN MIND, I'D BE TOO EMBARRASSED TO GO TO ONE THAT ANYONE ELSE HERE GOES TO...

I WASN'T FEELING SICK BEFORE, BUT NOW I HAVE A HEADACHE.

PROBABLY FROM CLENCHING YOUR TEETH. YOU'LL HAVE TO START ALL OVER WITH OUR DENTAL PLAN.

I WORRY ABOUT YOU BEING SICK AND ALL ALONE, CATHY.

I'M NOT SICK, MOM. I FEEL GREAT!

BUT IF YOU **WERE** SICK, YOU'D BE ALONE.

BUT I'M **NOT** SICK! MY WHOLE OFFICE GOT SICK, BUT I DIDN'T GET IT!

BUT YOU'LL **GET** SICK SOMETIME, AND YOU'LL BE ALL ALONE! NO ONE TO HELP YOU! NO ONE TO CARE FOR YOU! YOU'LL JUST BE LYING THERE, SICK AND ALONE!

AVOIDED 25,000,000 FLU GERMS. WAS FLATTENED BY AN AIRBORNE TRUTH PARTICLE.

LET DOWN THE WALLS! OPEN THE DOORS TO THE HEART! RADIATE LOVE AND LET LOVE COME POURING BACK TO YOU!

HI, THERE!

LATTE

AACK! PUT THE WALLS BACK UP! SHUT THE DOORS! BOLT THE WINDOWS! BARRICADE THE WHOLE AREA! AACK!

MIND IF I JOIN YOU?

NEVER UNLEASH THE EMOTIONAL RADAR BEFORE DOING A THOROUGH ROOM CHECK.

Guisewite

I DON'T KNOW WHAT IT WAS, BUT SOMETHING DREW ME TO SIT DOWN WITH YOU!

LATTE

...YES, WELL, I WAS EMANATING MY AURA OF AVAILABILITY, AND HAD JUST SENT IT TO THE HANDSOME MAN AT THE FRONT TABLE WHEN YOU WALKED BY AND INTERCEPTED IT WITH YOUR FAT STOMACH!

MY AURA OF AVAILABILITY IS NOW STUCK ON THE FRONT OF YOUR PLAID SHIRT! SHAKE IT OFF AND SEND IT OVER TO THE HUNK AT THE FRONT TABLE WHERE IT BELONGS!!

IT WAS AS IF SOMETHING HIT ME IN THE PIT OF THE STOMACH! I JUST CAN'T PUT IT INTO WORDS!

ME EITHER.

Guisewite

DON'T BE INSECURE! DON'T BE PARANOID!

DON'T BE JUDGMENTAL! DON'T REJECT ON LOOKS!

BE CONFIDENT! BE CARING!

BE CURIOUS! BE ACCESSIBLE!

RADIATE THE LIFE FORCE WITHIN AND LET HER SEE THE REAL YOU!

RELEASE PRECONCEPTIONS, AND BE AVAILABLE FOR MAGIC!

THE MODERN COUPLE: ONE HEART, ONE MIND, FIFTEEN SELF-HELP BOOKS.

OPEN YOUR HEART AND EMOTE!!

SHUT YOUR EYES AND FLIRT!!

Guisewite

...AND THEN...*Yawn*...AFTER COLLEGE, I... *Yawn*....

EXCUSE ME. I HAVE TO STOP AND ACKNOWLEDGE SOMETHING.

THIS IS THE LONGEST I'VE BEEN WITH A WOMAN IN THE LAST THREE YEARS, AND IT REPRESENTS A REAL BREAKTHROUGH FOR ME.

OF A BILLION STRANGERS WITH A BILLION AGENDAS, WHAT ARE THE CHANCES OF TWO PEOPLE MEETING AND SHARING WHAT WE HAVE TOGETHER ??

HERE'S TO OUR FIVE-MINUTE ANNIVERSARY!

AND HERE'S TO THE DESPERATE-FOR-ANY-HUMAN-CONNECTION DECADE.

I INITIATED CONTACT WITH A WOMAN, ENGAGED IN EMOTIONAL RISK-TAKING DIALOGUE FOR TWENTY MINUTES...AND NOW I'M GOING BACK TO MY MALE CAVE!

I WILL REFLECT, REGROUP, AND RE-ENERGIZE WHILE I SIT ALONE IN UTTER SILENCE AND COMPLETELY INACCESSIBLE SOLITUDE!

OK. BYE.

P.S. HERE'S MY CAVE'S PHONE NUMBER, CELL PHONE NUMBER, VOICE MAIL NUMBER, BEEPER NUMBER AND E-MAIL ADDRESS.

I HAVE LET GO OF ALL NEGATIVE JUDGMENTS ABOUT MY BODY, AND LOVINGLY ENVELOP IT IN SOFT, COZY FABRIC.

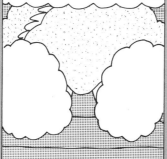
I HAVE RELEASED MY FEET FROM THE PRISON OF FOOTWEAR, AND SET THEM FREE IN BIG, FLUFFY SLIPPERS.

I'VE ACKNOWLEDGED MY DAY'S EFFORTS, AND AM HONORING MY NEED FOR QUIET, STRESS-FREE, NON-GOAL-ORIENTED DOWN TIME.

MARCH 1, 1997: REINVENTED SELF AS A THROW PILLOW.

AACK!! MY HAND!! I JUST WATCHED MY HAND PICK UP THE PHONE AND DIAL THE NUMBER OF A GEEKY MAN I MET AT A COFFEE SHOP!!

I FELT MY MOUTH OPENING! I HEARD MY VOICE ASK HIM OUT TO DINNER!!

I HAVE NO INTEREST IN HIM WHATSOEVER AND I JUST WITNESSED MYSELF GIGGLING AND ASKING HIM OUT!! WHAT'S GOING ON??!

...DEAR?

I'VE GIVEN UP ON MOTHERLY NUDGING AND HAVE MOVED INTO TELEKINESIS.

I CALLED A MAN I DO NOT WANT TO DATE AND ASKED HIM OUT... AND NOW I'M PUTTING ON MAKEUP FOR HIM!

IT'S MUSCLE MEMORY! I CAN'T STOP MYSELF! THE HAND DABS ON THE SULTRY EYE SHADOW... THE FINGERS GUIDE THE ALLURING LIPSTICK... THE ARMS REACH FOR THE SEDUCTIVE COLOGNE...

STOP FLUFFING! STOP PRIMPING! CAN'T YOU LOOK BAD NOW WHEN IT REALLY MATTERS?!

WOW!

RATS. AUTO-BEAUTY STRIKES AGAIN.

PASTA

THE MOMENT YOU CALLED, I VOWED TO DROP MY FAÇADE OF MANLY INDIFFERENCE, CATHY.

I'VE SPENT YEARS AS THE SILENT, DISTANT MALE...BUT TONIGHT, I BEGIN ANEW!

I WANT TO LISTEN! I WANT TO HEAR! I WANT TO OPEN UP! WE'RE TWO BRAND-NEW PEOPLE WITH TWO LIFETIMES OF EXPERIENCES TO SHARE!

YOUR TABLE WILL BE READY IN TEN MINUTES.

TEN MINUTES?? WHAT ARE WE SUPPOSED TO TALK ABOUT FOR TEN MINUTES??!

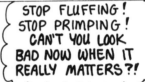

IT'S YOUR WEEK TO CLEAN UP THE COFFEE ROOM, CATHY.

FORGET IT. FRANK DIDN'T DO HIS TURN LAST WEEK. LOOK AT THIS MESS!

I DIDN'T DO MY WEEK BECAUSE IT WAS TOO BIG OF A MESS BECAUSE KIM DIDN'T DO HER WEEK!

I DIDN'T DO MY WEEK BECAUSE SUE DIDN'T DO HER WEEK BECAUSE TOM DIDN'T DO HIS WEEK!

I DIDN'T DO MY WEEK BECAUSE I FOLLOWED THE LEAD OF THE NINE FINE PROFESSIONALS BEFORE ME WHO DIDN'T DO THEIR WEEKS!

ANOTHER COMPANY REAPS THE REWARDS OF ITS MENTORING PROGRAM.

LET'S GO TO STARBUCKS! THEY HAVE CLEAN CUPS!

HOW AN OFFICE COPES WITH THE COFFEE ROOM IS A MICROCOSM OF ITS PRIDE, TEAM SPIRIT AND PROBLEM-SOLVING CAPABILITIES!

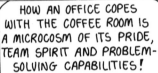

EVERYTHING OUR COMPANY IS TODAY AND WILL BE IN THE FUTURE EMANATES FROM WHAT HAPPENS IN THIS ONE LITTLE ROOM!

COFFEE ROOM

SO...WHAT HAPPENS IN THIS LITTLE ROOM, PEOPLE?

EVENTUALLY, ONE OF THE WOMEN GETS SO DISGUSTED, SHE CLEANS IT UP HERSELF.

HURRY UP AND HIT YOUR THRESHOLD. I NEED A CLEAN PLATE FOR MY BURRITO.

OUR CLIENT WILL BE HERE IN AN HOUR! WE KNOW WHAT WE HAVE TO DO, TEAM!

SHUT THE DOOR TO MY OFFICE SO THEY WON'T SEE THE MESS!

STUFF ALL THE DIRTY DISHES INTO THE REFRIGERATOR!

GRAB ALL THE JUNK IN THE CONFERENCE ROOM AND FLING IT IN THE COAT CLOSET!

SPRAY AIR FRESHENER AROUND TO COVER THE SMELL OF FRED'S LUNCH!

GO! GO! GO! GO!

SOME COMPANIES STRUT THEIR STUFF. WE TAKE PRIDE IN HOW WELL WE HIDE IT.

SQUIRT.

120

WHY'S EVERYONE STAND-ING AROUND?? OUR DEAD-LINE IS TOMORROW!

YAWN...WHAT'S A FEW MORE DAYS?

WE'VE BEEN KILLING OUR-SELVES ON THIS SINCE MON-DAY! WE CAN'T GIVE UP NOW!

YAWN...LET'S LET IT SLIDE UNTIL NEXT WEEK...

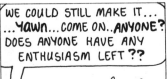

WE COULD STILL MAKE IT... ...YAWN...COME ON..ANYONE? DOES ANYONE HAVE ANY ENTHUSIASM LEFT??

YAWN

THURSDAY IS TO THE OFFICE WHAT 4:00PM IS TO THE DIET.

RING RING!

SHH! SETTLE DOWN! YOU'VE BEEN GOING NONSTOP SINCE 8:00AM!

RING RING!

SHH! PLEASE! JUST LET ME LOOK AT THIS FOR A SECOND!

RING RING RING!

QUIET! I CAN'T THINK! I CAN'T CONCENTRATE! QUIET!!!

HAVING FINALLY GOTTEN THE TELEPHONE DOWN FOR ITS AFTER-NOON NAP, ANOTHER CAREGIVER TACKLES HER TO-DO LIST.

THE WORLD WILL OPEN UP TO YOU WHEN YOU START GETTING OUT, CATHY.

I'VE BEEN OUT, MOM.

NOW I CAN'T GO BACK TO MY FAVORITE COFFEE SHOP BECAUSE I MIGHT RUN INTO A MAN I MET THERE A FEW WEEKS AGO...

I CAN'T GO BACK TO MY FAVORITE VIDEO STORE BE-CAUSE I MIGHT RUN INTO A MAN I MET THE WEEK BEFORE... I CAN'T GO TO THE GYM BECAUSE I MIGHT RUN INTO ALEX...I CAN'T GO TO MY NEIGHBORHOOD GROCERY STORE BECAUSE THAT'S WHERE NATHAN SHOPS...

HOW IS MY WORLD OPEN-ING UP? I CAN'T GO ANY-WHERE WITH-IN TEN MILES OF MY HOUSE!

YOU'RE BEING FORCED INTO NEW ZIP CODES!

WELCOME TO SPRING '97, AND THE MOST ROMANTIC NEW LOOKS IN YEARS!

WHISPER-THIN GAUZE DRESSES...SILKY SHEER SLIP TOPS...LACY, CROCHETED TUBE SKIRTS...

SPRING '97

ROMANCE IS BACK, AND WITH IT, THOSE THREE MAGICAL LITTLE WORDS...

SPRING '97

FULL BODY CORSET.

FOR MANY OF US, IT'S BEEN SO LONG...

I'M SICK OF WINTER, AND I'M SICK OF THIS BULKY, UGLY, HEAVY WINTER COAT!

BRING ME LIGHTNESS! BRING ME BREEZINESS! BRING ME SPRING ON A HANGER!

...AND NOW, BRING ME BACK MY COAT.

AACK!! I CAN SEE RIGHT THROUGH THIS DRESS!

YOU'RE NOT SUPPOSED TO WEAR IT ALONE, SILLY...

...SEE? LAYER THE SLIP DRESS OVER A BODYSUIT, UNDER A GAUZY TANK, UNDER A WISPY TEE, UNDER ANOTHER SLIP DRESS, UNDER A CHIFFONY WRAP-SKIRT, UNDER A FLOATY SHIFT, UNDER A BREEZY CAMISOLE, UNDER A DRAPEY JACKET...

...AND WHAT DO YOU HAVE??

A WAY TO TURN $3.00 OF FABRIC INTO A $750.00 SALE.

AACK!! SHE SAW RIGHT THROUGH THE SALES-CLERK!!

NOW THAT'S HUMILIATING!

THE BODY PART OF THE SEASON IS...

NOT THE TUMMY! NOT THE CHEST! NOT THE THIGH! NOT THE REAR!

SPRING '97

...THE SHOULDER!

THE SHOULDER?? I CAN DO THAT LOOK! I HAVE A LOVELY SHOULDER!!

THE SHOULDER! YES!! IT'S FINALLY MY YEAR! IT'S FINALLY MY SEASON! THANK YOU! THANK YOU!

HAS SHE SEEN THE KNITTED TUBE DRESS HER SHOULDER WILL BE STICKING OUT OF?

SH! DON'T RUIN MY SALE BY MENTIONING THE MERCHANDISE!

SPRING '97

THAT DRESS LOOKS COMPLETELY DIFFERENT WITH THE RIGHT UNDERWEAR... ..BUT ALL OUR UNDERWEAR IS ON THE THIRD FLOOR.

YOU CAN EITHER BUY THE DRESS AND TAKE IT UPSTAIRS TO TRY WITH THE UNDERWEAR...OR BUY THE UNDERWEAR AND BRING IT DOWN HERE TO TRY WITH THE DRESS.

YOU HAVE TO COMMIT TO SOMETHING OR NOTHING IS POSSIBLE! YOU HAVE TO JUST SHUT YOUR EYES, FORK OVER YOUR CHARGE CARD AND HOPE TO HIGH HEAVEN IT WON'T BE YET ANOTHER WRETCHED WASTE OF TIME AND MONEY!

OH, FINE. RING IT UP!

IF RELATIONSHIPS WITH MEN HAVE DONE NOTHING ELSE, AT LEAST THEY'VE PREPARED US TO SHOP.

JOGGING SUITS WE DIDN'T JOG IN...SWEAT SUITS WE DON'T SWEAT IN...ENOUGH! WE'VE FLOPPED IN FRONT OF THE TV IN EXERCISE-WEAR LONG ENOUGH!

PRO TRAIN

THIS SEASON WE RECLAIM OUR FEMININITY WITH CASUAL CLOTHES THAT TWIRL AND FLIRT FROM OUR TOES TO OUR SPARKLING TIARAS!

GOODBYE, COUCH ATHLETE. HELLO, COUCH BALLERINA.

IF WE'RE GOING TO VEGETATE, WHY NOT WEAR SOMETHING THAT INSPIRES PEOPLE TO THROW ROSES AT US?

BUY THE NEW OPEN-TOED, CHUNKY-SOLED STILETTO SANDALS, AND DOOM YOURSELF TO A SUMMER OF CRAMPED CALF MUSCLES, POTENTIAL ANKLE FRACTURES, WEEKLY PEDICURES AND DAILY HOSIERY NIGHTMARES AND/OR SELF-TANNING EPISODES!!

OK.

MY NEED FOR COMFORT IS EXCEEDED BY MY NEED TO OWN SOMETHING THAT SAYS "SIZE 7" ON IT.

"RETHINK THE DRESS..." "RETHINK THE DRESS..." WHY DID EVERYONE "RETHINK THE DRESS"? WE WERE HAPPY IN PANTS!

OH, WE STILL HAVE PANTS.

SEE? SKINNY, FLAT-FRONT STRETCH PANTS THAT REVEAL EVERY RIPPLE OF FLESH... OR FLOWING TRANSPARENT TULLE PANTS THAT REVEAL EVERY RIPPLE OF FLESH...

...BOTH WORN WITH SQUISHY TOPS OR CROPPED JACKETS THAT END ONE INCH ABOVE THE WIDEST PART OF THE REAR!

I BELIEVE I'LL RETHINK THE DRESS.

IT'S JUST A MATTER OF TIME BEFORE THE SHOPPERS ARE IN SYNC WITH THE DESIGNERS.

I CAN'T WEAR A CHIFFON DRESS AND SPARKLY SANDALS TO THE OFFICE!!

WHY NOT?

WOMEN HAVE PAID OUR DUES IN THE WORKPLACE! WE DON'T HAVE TO LIVE BY THAT ANCIENT, BORING MALE DRESS CODE ANYMORE!

OUR VOICES ARE BEING HEARD... NOW, LET OUR INDIVIDUALITY BE SEEN! LET'S SHOW MEN WHAT A REAL INDEPENDENT DECISION-MAKER LOOKS LIKE!!

A FAIRY GODMOTHER.

HOW MUCH MORE EMPOWERED CAN YOU GET??

THIS SPRING WE CELEBRATE THE RETURN TO FEMININITY!

WHAT FEMININITY?

GREAT GRANDMA WAS UP AT 4:00AM MILKING COWS... ...GRANDMA SCRUBBED FLOORS AND WASHED SHEETS BY HAND... MOM RACED BETWEEN A PART-TIME JOB AND FULL-TIME MOTHERHOOD...

WHEN WAS THE FEMININITY WE'RE RETURNING TO?? WHAT WOMAN EVER HAD TIME TO LOOK THIS DAINTY??

1892: CHLOE SMIRKLE HAD A 15-SECOND CHAOS-FREE WINDOW WHERE SHE STROLLED IN THE GARDEN WEARING A SLIP JUST LIKE THIS!

HER NORMAL CLOTHES WERE ALL IN THE HAMPER.

I SEE THAT "SECRETARIES' WEEK," WHICH USED TO BE A WEEK, HAS BEEN DOWNSIZED TO "SECRETARIES' DAY."

TUESDAY OF WHAT USED TO BE OUR WEEK, HAS BECOME "EARTH DAY," AND THURSDAY IS NOW "TAKE OUR DAUGHTERS TO WORK DAY."

WHY DO I GET THE FEELING YOU KEPT WEDNESDAY TO HONOR THE DWINDLING SECRETARIAL POOL ONLY SO YOU'LL HAVE US IN A HAPPY MOOD THAT DAY TO CLEAN UP FROM TUESDAY AND DECORATE FOR THURSDAY?!

A GOOD SECRETARY DOES THE JOB. A GREAT ONE ANTICIPATES.

WELCOME TO EARTH DAY '97, AND SHAME ON YOU.

AS OF 10:00AM, OUR "WHITE PAPER ONLY" BIN CONTAINED 3 HALF-EATEN BREAKFAST BURRITOS, 19 PLASTIC SPOONS, 12 TAKE-OUT COFFEE CUPS, 7 VICTORIA'S SECRET CATALOGS, 5 SOFT DRINK CANS, 4 AAA BATTERIES, A BROKEN PENCIL SHARPENER, AND A BREATH SPRAY SQUIRTER.

IT'S JIM'S FAULT!
IT'S MARCIA'S FAULT!
IT'S JOHN'S FAULT!
IT'S CINDY'S FAULT!
IT'S TIM'S FAULT!
IT'S SUE'S FAULT!
IT'S YOUR FAULT!

WE'VE ABANDONED THE ECOSYSTEM, BUT WE'VE MANAGED TO PRESERVE THE ECHO-SYSTEM.

THE BUSINESS WOMAN IN THE CONFIDENCE-EXUDING LINGERIE SLIP AND MATTE JERSEY SPORTCOAT!

THE BUSINESS WOMAN IN THE WINNING ATTITUDE ELONGATED TOGA TUBE TOP AND DIMPLE KNIT SKIRT!

THE BUSINESS WOMAN IN THE NO-NONSENSE SEQUINED CAMISOLE AND MEADOW-PRINT FLIP SKIRT!

THE BUSINESS WOMAN IN THE OFFICE LADIES' ROOM ON THE CELL PHONE:

HELLO! I DEMAND TO SPEAK TO MY SALES-PERSON!